Memorial Road

WWII Memoirs of Corporal John Calvin Estes, T5

1st Army of the United States, 3rd Division, 7th Corp., Company B, 49th
Combat Engineer Group,
Good Conduct Medal
World War II Victory Medal

Five Bronze Service Stars

Normandy Northern France Ardennes Rhineland Central Europe

As Told To Ginger Ausban Povelites

Memorial Road
Published by Yawn's Publishing
210 East Main Street
Canton, GA 30114
www.yawnspublishing.com

Library of Congress Control Number: 2011942978

ISBN13: 978-1-936815-31-9

Printed in the United States

Introduction

Some men are not meant for fame or fortune. They don't possess that alluring charm that attracts the multitudes of followers nor do they have the need to accumulate great monetary wealth. Their names won't go down in history books, there won't be a holiday celebrated in their honor nor will their faces be painted on US currency. I see these ordinary men in places like church on Sunday, the local grocery store and in the city park. These unsung heroes are the backbone of our great nation and without them it would not exist.

In most cases, veterans of past wars don't expect to be recognized for their honor and valor other than their earned military medals and rewards. They have laid their lives on the line for freedom simply because they thought it was their duty. To most it doesn't matter that cheers are not greeting them everywhere they go.

It took sixty years for this country to give World War II veterans a memorial in our nation's capital, and the delay has surely eaten a hole in the heart of our greatest generation. During these sixty years, many have tried to forget the war but have failed. Others hang on to those memories as a living memorial to their fallen buddies. For the few that are still living, I suspect that in most cases the memories are as fresh today as they were the moment after they happened.

If you know a living member of this "should be honored society", I urge you to go to him or her, get a tape recorder or video recorder, put it in front of that person, turn it on, and ask the question, "Could you tell me some war stories?" Then sit back and really listen. I'm sure the stories will start to flow. Maybe you are like me who, as a young person didn't want to listen or you were too busy. Time is running out, and you must act now!

Looking back I remember that growing up in the south during the 1950 and 1960's was carefree except for an occasional bout with my pesky younger brother. There were times when I'd find myself trapped in adult conversations which were frequently about the war. Time and time again I would get caught up in what I thought was an impossibly boring situation. Once I was trapped I would wait for a chance to escape. While trying to figure out how to break free I'd ask myself, "How the heck am I going to get out of here?" At the same time I didn't want to hurt anybody's feelings because I was a polite young southern lady. After all, they sure did sound like they were enjoying the conversation. Minutes that seemed like hours would pass, and somehow I would manage to sneak away and get back to more important things like catching lightening bugs in the back yard.

Weekend gatherings would always lead to the men in the family sitting around on the porch drinking beer while my Grandmother, Mary and my Mom, Viola, and any number of aunts would clean up after a large southern meal. My cousins, siblings and I would run endlessly in and out of the house. Randy, my brother, would yell, "Look! The lightening bugs are out!"

I would say, "I'll go see if Mary's got a jar we can use to catch 'em. I'll be right back." It never failed. I'd get the jar and run out of the house trying to fly past the adults, and my dad's arm would come out and grab me. "Hey girl, where're you going? Give me a hug." Before I knew it one of the men would say something to me, and all of a sudden I'd find myself trapped in the boring old adult conversation. Most of the time the men in the group would continue to talk, telling those dumb old war stories while passing around some old guns. They'd show me the guns and say something about where they came from, as if I was interested! Darn it anyway, I felt obligated to stay by my daddy's side until there was a break in the conversation.

I'd try to pay attention, even though I worried that my annoying little brother might be out there squishing fireflies just to see the green glow on his hand. But what in the world were they talking about anyway? I didn't understand a thing. What was a half-track? Who was Big Bertha? I just wanted to get back in the yard with the jar. Finally, someone would go get more beer, and I would be out of there before the lid could be opened on the cooler.

Dumb old war stories; who cared about that stuff anyway? All anyone had to do was go to the drive-in, and before the cartoon came on, see with his or her very own eyes film footage about the war. On the big screen, it looked kind of interesting with all those big guns and smoke and buildings blowing up. Besides all that neat stuff, what was there to cause my Grandfather, Calvin, to go on and on and on. My Grandmother, Mary, said it was the beer. She didn't seem to like it when Calvin started telling those stories, but the men sure did seem to enjoy them. They would laugh and laugh, and one time I thought I caught Calvin with a tear in his eye.

As the years flew by I was always too busy to listen. While I worked and raised a family time passed, and the war stories dried up along with the tears and laughter. Recently my Grandmother passed away. With her passing, I got to spend some quality time with my Grandfather, whom I have called Calvin for all my life. One day I asked, "Calvin, how come you don't tell war stories anymore?"

He said, "Mary didn't like it too much."

I thought it was the beer she didn't like and the war stories were associated with the beer drinking. Maybe she didn't like being reminded of something else or maybe she just didn't like Calvin remembering those bad times.

Now, since I'm a Grandmother myself, I have been feeling kind of nostalgic and curious. So I looked at him and said, "Tell me a war story." That's all I had to say. The stories started flowing, and I couldn't believe what I was hearing. My mouth dropped open with disbelief. I laughed and I wanted to cry. I started taking notes, but there was just too much. My note taking was not getting it all down, and I ran out of time, so I scheduled a special visit. This time I was prepared with a tape recorder and plenty of blank tape cartridges. Calvin has such incredible memories of a sad and terrifying time that happened sixty years ago, and I wanted to hear all of them. In the beginning of this project, most of the stories he told me where the ones he has told over and over again, but as I dug deep into his memory, I uncovered other stories that he has not spoken of since the day they happened.

According to the World Book Encyclopedia, in World War II over ten million American and allied soldiers were killed and over six million soldiers from Germany and its allied countries known as the axis countries were also killed. In addition, during this time known as the Holocaust, over six million Jews and Polls lost their lives. Think about it: that's a total of approximately twenty-two million lives lost over a period of six years. It's hard to imagine the monstrosity of such an event especially when we compare it to the wars being fought today.

Not knowing what he was getting into, this young, hardworking family man, practical joker, and volunteer from the state of Tennessee gave up his deferment status and joined the Army to help his President. In doing so, he trained as a combat engineer and received Army Ranger training. He moved to the front line on D-Day, June 6, 1944, in Normandy and kept his feet on the ground touring Europe through occupation until December 9, 1945.

During this time period he fought in five major battles: Normandy, Northern France, Ardennes, Rhineland and Central Europe. In the middle of it all, he spent thirty days in a mental hospital in England while suffering from battle fatigue. After his hospital stay he refused to accept limited duty as an MP and asked to be returned to his outfit. When he couldn't go home, he insisted on rejoining his buddies, as he called them, on the front line in Germany where they broke through and infiltrated behind the Nazi line. As part of small task force of the First Army, he spearheaded through Germany and became a liberator of Nazi concentration camps.

Before the end of the war he robbed a Nazi owned bank (taking what is estimated to be worth over thirteen million in present day dollars) and during the occupation used part of the money to help a war devastated German town rebuild its industry. He survived numerous deadly situations but suffered only a scratch and a small case of scabies and returned home penniless.

This book is not intended to be a documentation of the history of World War II but a story of the experiences faced by a "damn good soldier", whose objective was to do his job, survive the conflict, and return home to his family.

Come join with me, and experience the human side of this most hideous time in history as told by John Calvin Estes.

Four Stages of a Soldier: While in Active Duty

First Stage: Top dog

He feels like he's the best damn soldier in the world. After receiving the best kill and destroy training in the world, he's tough, motivated and ready to fight.

Second Stage: Scared

During the top dog stage, many will die and the survivors will get scared. Reality sets in that it's not a game and he also could die. He realizes that the enemy is just as good a soldier as he is and just as vulnerable.

Third Stage: Doesn't Care

Once a soldier reaches the third stage, he has seen more of his buddies get hit and realizes the odds of surviving are very poor. When he reaches the point of not caring and wants to take with him as any of the sons-of-bitches that he can, then this is when he's really the BEST soldier.

Fourth Stage: Careful

After surviving a few months of active combat, the soldier starts to think, "I've made it this far. It would be ashamed to get bumped off at the last minute." So he gets careful because he realizes he just might make it home after all.

It's a hard life,

John C. Estes

Chapter 1 - Greetings

Jew Joe is what I called him all my life. I was raised up with him and his older brother, Isaac in West Nashville. We played ball together out in the streets of College Park, went to school together and were best buddies. During the depression my family moved to Smithville, Tennessee where I learned to enjoy living on my grandparents' (Dave and Mary Miller) farm and fishing and hunting. On this farm at a place called Dry Creek, is where I learned how to handle firearms and I became an avid outdoorsman. My family returned to Nashville in about 1935, when I was twelve years old. My dad opened Estes' Grocery, a corner grocery store on 12th Avenue North. A couple of years later I ran into Joe and Isaac again because they ran a Standard Sales outfit and sold notions to stores. Jew Joe serviced my dad's store.

I met my lovely bride of fifty-six years, Mary Ellen Wilson, on a blind date in early 1941. Her best friend, Doris, was dating J.B., a friend of mine who fixed us up. The first time I saw her she was climbing into the back seat of a 1936 Ford to sit next to me while on a double date. She was the most beautiful girl I had ever seen with her long auburn hair. That night we just rode around town and ended up at Shelby Park. While we were sitting there in the car a discussion came up about the New Testament. It just so happened that J.B. had a Bible in the glove compartment. He turned on the dome light and started reading the New Testament. We must have parked the car in a restricted area because about that time a police officer came walking up shining his flashlight through the open car window. The only thing we could see was a big bright light as the officer's authoritative voice cut through the darkness and asked, "What are you doing here?" He was moving the flashlight beam all around the car including the back seat.

J.B. answered, "Why officer, we're reading the Bible."

"Yea, sure you are."

"See here." J.B. then holds the Bible up to the officer's light.

"Well, I guess you are." The officer was surprised. "But let's move on anyway." J.B. started the car and we drove out of the park. I did manage to sneak a kiss or two before we dropped the girls off. That night I told J.B., "That's the girl I'm going to marry".

Mary and I fell in love at the 1941 Tennessee State Fair and were married on March 7, 1942. We rented a little house next door to my parent's house. Their names were Charlie and Lizzie Estes. Mary already had a ten-year-old daughter named Viola when we married, and she is the only child I ever had.

Mary with 32 Ford

Mary didn't know how to drive a car and didn't want to learn. But I kept pushing her to get behind the wheel, so she finally gave it a try. I taught her how to drive my car, which had the first V8 engine ever made; it was a sky blue 1932 B Model Ford. Even after she got her driver's license she absolutely did not like driving and would only do so when I insisted.

With a family to support I trained as a welder and at the age of twenty I went to work for The Nashville Bridge Company in early 1943. There I built PT boats and barges. I had reached "first class welder" status when the draft deal first called me. However, because of my contribution to the war effort by building boats, I received a six-month deferment.

All my buddies were shipping out. I tried to convince myself that I was helping the war effort. I even donated a day's pay to the American Red Cross to support their effort in helping troops during the war. But the little things I was doing didn't overcome my feeling of guilt when I'd see other guys in uniforms kissing their loved ones goodbye. I felt so bad about not going that I didn't turn my card back in when it came time for another deferment. I didn't tell Mary what I had done and she naturally assumed that I had turned it back in.

"Greetings, your President needs your help." That's what the letter said in the mail that day when Mary opened it. She got really upset with me and wasn't very happy about it because I was called in to service when we had only been married for a little over a year. Also, she was very sickly at that time and really needed me at home. Not to mention the fact that she didn't like the idea of driving herself everywhere she needed to go after having the luxury of a husband-chauffeur.

The letter from President Franklin D. Roosevelt said to report to the local induction center in Smyrna, Tennessee

4

on August 8, 1943 for my physical examination. I really did want to do my patriotic duty and help my President, so I gladly followed the instructions in the letter and reported to the induction center.

There were several guys reporting at the same time. We were sent into a physical examination room to take medical tests. We had to strip down or get completely naked and stand in line. The medical examiner said to the first guy in line, "See those jars on the wall over there?"

The first guy said, "Yea."

"Take a piss in one."

"From over here?" asked the first guy.

"I wonder how many times I've heard that one? Just go take a piss and when you're done we're going to do a short arm inspection."

A "short arm inspection" is where the soldiers' gentiles are examined for ruptures and diseases. I guess the exam is to make sure it's working properly. First, the naked soldiers form a line in front of a doctor who usually sits on a stool. Then, when each soldier steps forward the doctor will say, "Skin it back and milk it down." As the soldier skins it back pus will come out if Gonorrhea is present. The whole experience was pretty funny to most of us, and we started cracking jokes about the procedure.

After the physical examination was over and the paperwork was complete, I sat down in front of a desk and across from the induction officer. As I sat watching, he looked over my paperwork and said, "Well, boy, we're going to put you in the Marines."

I got excited and said, "No! I don't want the Marines. I want the Army!"

"Why?"

"I hear the Army gives a thirty day leave and the Marines only give two weeks."

He asked, "What the hell's wrong with the Marines?"

"Listen bud, I don't know anything about either one of them but my wife is sick and I need the thirty days."

He hesitated then said, "Okay. The Army it is, if you're sure that's what you want." I was immediately sworn in as an Army soldier.

I got the thirty days leave so I could make sure Mary was okay. She was having female problems. During this leave we went to see a movie at the Knickerbocker Theater in Nashville. The first thing that was shown was always a film about the war. And on this day they were showing a bunch of ships crossing the Atlantic and going through a terrific storm. The bows of the ships were going plum under the water. I said to Mary, "That's unbelievable. If I have to go across, I hope to see something like that." Even though I knew I would miss Mary, I was getting excited about my new adventure and looked forward to getting it over with at the same time.

At the end of the thirty days I boarded a troop train headed for Chattanooga. When we arrived at the Chattanooga station, a truck picked us up and took us to the Army induction center at Fort Oglethorpe, Georgia. We arrived after dark and hadn't eaten, so we went to the mess hall. There was a big sign on the wall that said, "Take what you want, but eat what you take." After breakfast the next morning, we were fitted and issued uniforms. We were not allowed to keep any personal items. What clothing I wore on the first day had to be thrown away or returned home. I mailed my clothing and other personal items home to Mary.

We went back into the barracks and changed into our uniforms and then gathered outside. A platoon sergeant shouted, "Line up, arm's length." We marched over to a testing facility where I went through a process of taking tests and being interviewed about what I did in civilian life. During this process I ran into Jew Joe and Isaac.

"Hey, Johnny! Surprised to see you here."

"Jew Joe! Isaac! What are you doing here?"

"We're in charge. We're non-coms, non-commissioned officers. We handle everything in here. We route people to the right place, make assignments, give test and all that kind of stuff."

My friends did me a big favor that day. They didn't assign me to the regular infantry. They held me at Fort Oglethorpe for almost three weeks waiting for enough troops to fill a combat engineer outfit. I'm sure that my welding experience played a big factor in their decision, and I was happy about the assignment.

During my stay at Fort Oglethorpe, every time I went into the PX the jukebox was playing, Pistol Packing Mama.

Drinking beer in a cabaret
And was I having fun
Until one night she caught me right
And now I'm on the run.
Oh! Lay that pistol down, Babe.
Lay that pistol down!
Pistol packing mama,
Lay that pistol down.

Chapter 2 - Special Training

After hanging around Fort Oglethorpe for about three weeks, the non-coms got enough soldiers to fill a combat engineer group. We were put on a troop train headed to Fort Leonard Wood, Missouri, which is about sixty miles outside of St. Louis. At Ft. Oglethorpe I met an old soldier who told me to always volunteer to do guard duty in the mess car when I get on a troop train. He said that way I would always get plenty to eat. So I volunteered to be the guard on the mess car and what he said was true. I had plenty to eat.

We stopped at a train depot in Nashville and we were held there for two hours. They wouldn't let me off the train to call my wife. She had just visited me on the Sunday before I left, but I didn't know how long it would be before I would see her again. So I wrote her a letter and gave it to a Car Knocker to mail. A Car Knocker is what they call someone who greases the bearings on the trains or pours oil in the journal boxes (the axle). He did mail the letter because later Mary wrote to me and said she had received my letter.

We arrived at Fort Leonard Wood on a Thursday and were called to line up almost immediately. Captain Bell wanted to introduce himself and briefly meet each one of us. I was standing next to a couple of Mexicans. I think their names were Carlos and Emanuel. Captain Bell asked Carlos, "Where are you from soldier?"

Carlos answered in broken English, "See, I from Mexico City."

"How did you get in the Army?"

"I been live down in Texas and got a letter."

"I see." Then Captain Bell stepped in front of Emanuel and asked, "What's your name soldier and where are you from?"

Oct. 18/43

Dearest Darling wife,

I will answer the 2
air mail letters I recieved
last night was glad to get
them hon, I sure hope you
got home alright I made it
just fine you said something
about a short letter hon when
you get a short letter I just
don't have time to rite a long
one. Hon I sure did enjoy my
self sunday I sure hated to
leave you not knowing how
long it would be before I
could see you again hon, Hon
if I don't see you for a while
be sweet and don't worry I
Will be alright, I am fixing

9

two take a long ride now babe I hope it is clouer to tome. Hon I am leaving at 11.30 this morning I guess I am going north by the clocks Well hon I have got to get ready to go so I had litter close, hon I will call you when I get there if I can. hon I love you babe
  Well be sweet and I will do the same your Darling
  husband Calvin

Emanuel just kind of looked at the Captain and turned is head and sequenced his eyes.

"Soldier, I asked you a question."

Then Emanuel said, "No comprende`."

"God Damn it! Can't they send me soldiers that can speak English? This is ridiculous. Sergeant get this man out of here."

Ole Carlos's mouth flew open but he didn't say anything. Then the Captain came to me. He gave me a hard look. I guess because I look as Mexican as the two fellows he had just spoken to he thought he was going to have to reassign me as well. The Captain leaned in close to me and asked, "Well soldier, do you speak English?"

"Yes sir. I'm John Estes from Tennessee."

"Thank goodness." Then he moved on down the line to address the other fellows.

We were then issued our equipment and M1 rifles that they called "pieces". We were told to memorize all serial numbers; our dog tag number, rifle number and bayonet number. We were instructed to clean all pieces and to get them ready for the inspection that would be on the following Saturday.

When we were back in the barracks ole Carlos said, "Damn it. Me don't think too good! Why don't think of that?" He was ranting and raving.

I asked, "What are you talking about?"

"Ole Emanuel speak good English as me!" I just laughed about it as Carlos went around kicking the bunk legs and acting pissed.

That Saturday morning they announced over the intercom system, "Fall out for inspection!" That meant get out of the barracks and line up in your specified squad position, standing at attention and holding your piece down at your side. Then our Captain, Captain Bell, with the platoon sergeant at his side, started at the beginning of the row from left to right and stepped in front of the first

11

soldier and turned to face him. Immediately, the soldier was to bring his piece up to port arms. Port arms is the inspection position where the end of the barrel is up at a forty-five degree angle and always pointing to the left. The left hand is on the barrel and the right hand is on the stock. The Captain would take his right hand and slap the piece and take it from the soldier for inspection.

So Captain Bell was going down the line looking at the rifles and all troops in the line were gigged for dirty rifles until he got to me.

He announced, "Here's the piece I've been looking for."

My first thought was, "Oh hell what have I done now?"

He stepped out in front of the platoon holding my piece and passed it down to every one of the troops and said, "Take a good look at that piece. Take a long hard look at everything about that piece. There will be another inspection in two hours and all of your pieces better look like this one."

Then he stepped back in front of me and asked, "Where did you say you're from, soldier?"

"I'm from Tennessee, sir."

"Do you do a lot of hunting?"

"Yes sir!"

He then presented the rifle to me. I was feeling really good and proud at that time. I slapped the rifle with my left hand showing my finger nails directly at him. My index finger has a bum nail with an old injury and looks dirty all the time and there's nothing I can do about it. But when he saw the bad nail he said, "Sergeant, gig that man for a dirty finger nail."

I then thought to myself, "Oh hell, there's no way to win."

Getting a gig was not a good thing. It meant you had to pull some kind of extra duty like doing KP (kitchen patrol) or cleaning toilets. The Captain was all the time trying to gig you. During inspections he would walk around behind you and tell you to raise your right foot. He would inspect the sole of you boot. Then he would tell you to raise your left foot. Naturally, you would have to put your right foot down to raise your left foot and when you did, he'd gig you because he didn't tell you to put your right foot down.

If he caught you throwing down a cigarette butt, he'd gig you. Sometimes he'd make you dig a six by six by six-foot hole and then bury the cigarette butt. Once it was buried he'd ask which direction the mouthpiece was pointed and if you couldn't tell him, you'd have to dig it up to find out.

I never did have to dig a six by six-foot hole because I knew how to take care of my butts. We had to stripe all the paper off from around the butt, wad the paper in to a little ball and break the tobacco up. Then it could be thrown down on the ground and no one could see it.

The Captain would try to fool us any chance he got. For example, he would take someone's bayonet for inspection and ask for the rifle number. We had to respond quickly, and if we shouted out the bayonet number instead of the rifle number by accident, then we were gigged. The sergeant was always nearby taking down names of those getting the gig.

Anytime our foot hit the ground no matter where we were going, to the mess hall or for inspection or to the rifle range, it didn't matter, we had to be running. There was no walking. Captain Bell said that we'd find out why at the end of our training.

I went right into my special training as a combat engineer. My total training lasted seventeen weeks. Not all-combat engineers received demolition training or ranger training, but these were a major part of my special training. Demolition training consisted of learning to handle all kinds of explosives. I also learned how to build bailey bridges and pontoon bridges. A bailey bridge is a steel bridge that comes in sections and either you pin, bolt or clamp them together to expand across an area on land or water. A pontoon bridge uses pontoons to float wooden or steel expansions on water.

Ranger training which I believe is equivalent to today's Special Forces training, is where you learn to infiltrate behind enemy lines by climbing trees, walking on top of buildings, and moving through fields, streets and buildings quietly and quickly. I learned how to dress where I couldn't be noticed or heard or seen so I could slip up on someone. We'd wear a soft hat instead of a helmet and shoes with no buckles instead of combat boots. We only carried a colt 45 in a soft holster and a trench knife; just a very thin blade about six inches long. I practiced reconnaissance, the art of sneaking around in the dark to find out where the enemy is located. During this special training I learned how to take out enemy soldiers without making a noise by using the trench knife or something like bailing wire. We practiced on dummies.

WWII was mostly man on man or hand to hand combat unlike the high tech stuff they use today.

We learned transition firing. An example of transition firing is walking around at night and hearing a noise then firing from the hip towards the noise.

The hardest part of this training was bayonet training. It lasted for about a week. The training officers had wired together several two-inch thick sticks to form several dummy targets about the size of a man's body. We practiced charging the dummies and sticking them with our bayonets. We practiced "pairing off". This is what they call the technique used to keep you from getting stuck by an enemy bayonet. It was sort of like sword fighting but using a rifle with a bayonet on the end. On the last day of bayonet training the instructor asked, "Would any one like to challenge me?"

No one said anything, and then I asked, "Are you kidding?"

14

"No, I'm not kidding. You can try to stick me but I'll only pair you off."

"Okay, I'll challenge you."

We started fighting with the bayonets and I was really trying to stick him in the belly. But he just used his bayonet to pair me off and I never could stick him.

Another thing we were taught was how to fire a rifle grenade. You would attach a grenade launcher to the end of your rifle and using a blank cartilage you could take a small tank out if you had to. That thing would really kick. It'd put you back on your butt it kicked so hard.

I wanted to learn as much as I could to protect my unit and myself.

I believe I got picked for demolition school because one day I was standing in the aisle of the barracks when the Lieutenant and Sergeant walked in. All of a sudden the Sergeant pitched a quarter pound of TNT and a stick of dynamite at me. He had pitched them a pretty good ways towards me and I made an extra effort to catch the dynamite and let the TNT fall to the floor. I didn't know at the time but the dynamite was a dummy. The Lieutenant asked, "Why did you do that?"

"Well, this dynamite takes a twenty five pound jar to put it off, and that TNT takes a detonator cap to put it off."

"Good, step over here. You're in demolition school."

I became familiar with dynamite while living on my Grandparent's farm. My uncle supervised a road gang during the depression, and he kept dynamite in the barn all the time. His son and I played around with a stick because we wanted to hear the boom. We took a half stick and poked a hole in the dynamite and stuck in a cap with a fuse. We put it on a stump in front of my grandparents' house, struck a match to the fuse and took off running. The force of the blast threw us to the ground and I could hear glass shattering. When I opened my eyes I was happy to see the house was still standing with only a couple of windows blown out. We got into so much trouble that day.

On the first day of demolition school we went out to a portion of a railroad track that was used for practice. The instructor put a quarter pound of TNT on that railroad track. Then he took a six-pound sledgehammer and he hit it as hard as he could, but it didn't put it off. It just powdered up just like you'd hit a bunch of powder. He said he just wanted to show us what it takes to put off TNT.

Composition C was another explosive that we received training on. Now I think they call the same thing, plastic explosives. It looked like kid's play dough and came in a block. We would pinch off a piece, mash it up; it was soft and we would roll it up to about the size of your middle finger. We could just stick it around a railroad track iron. I believe we were practicing on a ninety-pound rail. We would stick it on the rail and stagger it just a little bit and set it off with a regular detonator cap. It would cut that rail just like it had been sawed.

The job of a combat engineer was to go in ahead of the infantry and armored divisions to clear minefields and bridge gaps enabling our forces to advance. When the infantry had passed, the engineers constructed obstacles, set mines and destroyed bridges to stop the enemy from coming in from behind.

I got only two seventy-two hour passes during the entire seventeen weeks of training. There was no time to go home for a visit because it was a long drive by car, bus or train from Fort Leonard Wood, Missouri to Nashville, Tennessee. Besides that the bus and train tickets were expensive and Mary couldn't afford to take off from work, and of course, she was afraid to drive. She wrote to me almost every day, therefore, mail call was always a special time.

I made friends with Fugua, who was also from Nashville. His wife could drive so one time Mary caught a ride up with Fugua's wife to visit.

Because my buddies and me wouldn't have much to do but hang out on the weekends we were always trying to get a card game going. We needed at least four or five people to play poker. I loved a good card game and would bug people to play. There was this one guy who was reluctant to play. He was one of the most country-boy looking guys I've ever seen. He had red hair and freckles and was from Little Rock, Arkansas.

"Hey, Red! You want to play?"

"No, I sure don't", he'd say until one day I guess he got tired of me bugging him.

"Come on Little Rock, it's just a harmless card game. Can I deal you in?"

"Okay, I'll play with you but I won't deal the cards."

"Well, why not?"

"If you must know, I can't keep from handling them and setting the cards. I'll control the cards one-way or the other. And I can't help it."

"What do you mean?"

"I was born and raised in a gambling house in Arkansas."

Well that card game was thrown aside because we wanted to see what he could do. So he shuffled the cards and passed the cards for me to cut them. So I did a "whore house" cut. That's what you call a cut when the cards are cut three ways. He dealt them out while all of us were really watching him closely.

He said, "Now this game will be for jacks or better. When I'm through dealing the cards, each one of you will be able to open."

And sure enough, each one of us could open with jacks or better.

"So someone go ahead and open and each one of you draw your cards just like you would if you were playing for money." So we drew the cards.

Then he said, "Now all of you would bet and you'd stay in the game. You've all got a pretty good hand, except mine is just a little bit better."

So he did that two or three times, and we were watching him and trying to catch him, but we never did catch him. He told us that he could read any Bicycle brand cards and that he could also control dice. Well, of course, we had to see that too.

"Anybody can control dice on a pool table or a blanket," He said.

"I can't", I said.

"The hardest place to control dice is on concrete. So let's go into the latrine and I'll show you." The latrine had concrete floors.

So he took the dice, "I'm going to start at snake eyes, go up to boxcars, and then go back to snake eyes."

He was bucking the dice up against the wall and he went to snake eyes, up to boxcars, and back down to snake eyes. I think he missed only once. He was good. So he never would join in on a card game. He said he didn't want to take our money.

The night before the last day of training, Captain Bell announced over the "bitch box", our name for the two-way intercom system, "Fall out in the morning for a forced march. Tomorrow we're going to separate the men from the boys. Be dressed and with full combat ready pack." That meant we had to have on our regular fatigue uniform and GI combat boots. We were to carry our combat pack, which included our shelter half (one-half of an Army tent), blanket, tent pegs and mess gear. We also had to have our rifle, canteen and gas mask.

Our Sergeant told us that a whole bunch of guys didn't make the entire march during the last training session.

18

Everybody in the barracks was sitting around talking about how they thought they'd handle it. Ole Fugua said, "John, I don't think you're going to make it."

I said with a big question mark, "You think you will?"

"Hell yea!"

"Well, I'll bet you that you don't make it and I will."

That night I bet a month's pay with Fugua that I'd make the twenty-two mile march and he wouldn't.

Before breakfast the next morning we started the march. Captain Bell was leading the pack along with all the platoon officers. They told us when to run and when to quickstep, which was about one hundred and twenty paces per minute. We'd run five minutes and quickstep five minutes. We were running through a mountainous area around Big Piney and Little Piney Rivers. After a few miles, guys started dropping out. About half way we heard a jeep coming up behind us. I turned around and saw that he was spraying tear gas right out the side of his jeep. We had to get our gas mask on quick or we would have choked. Out of forty-five in my platoon only ten made it all the way. I don't think I would have made it if it hadn't been for that bet. The bet was off because ole Fugua felt the same way and he made it too. I told the Captain after the march, "That was not training that was punishment."

After the march we were in the barracks cleaning up and getting ready for breakfast when the Captain announced over the bitch box that the mess hall was going to serve us real eggs that morning. Everybody got all excited and rushed to the mess hall. We were excited because we had been eating powdered eggs during our entire training and were going to get something special. There was nothing I liked better than fresh scrambled eggs, so I anxiously got in line. Then I laid my eyes on the eggs behind the serving line. They looked kind of raw so surely they hadn't cooked them yet.

19

Johnny in full combat pack

But then to my surprise, the cooks started slopping the eggs on the plates as the plates were being hesitantly held forward. The guy in front of me stuck out his plate and the mess cook slapped two eggs down. They were definitely sunny side up and running clear. The GI said, "I ain't going to eat that!"

The mess cook said, "I don't care if you eat it or not. Now move on."

So I didn't say a word. I stuck my plate up and accepted the two eggs. He might as well have just cracked them over my plate. My mother and Mary had always cooked me hard-cooked, fried, or scrambled eggs. I'd never eaten anything like that before. But I was starving to death after the forced march and the first bite was real hard to swallow.

Then I figured out how to sop my bread in my plate and it turned out to taste pretty good.

The next day we understood our training was over, and we were relieved and looking forward to rest after the forced march. But early that morning the bitch box came on and the first sergeant announced, "Fall out, we've got to go pull targets for C Company."

Murdock, a guy from Memphis got right up at the bitch box and said, "Go to hell!"

"Who said that?"

"Murdock, by god." He was pissed off. Then the whole barracks shouted, "That goes for all of us too!"

Then a few minutes later, Captain Bell came on the intercom and said, "Listen fellows, we owe C Company a target pull that was rained out the other day. They pulled for us. So we owe them and don't need to shirk our duty." We were pissed off about it because we thought we were done and we knew pulling targets was hard work.

We got up and did our duty, but that meant a five-mile march out, sitting in a ditch all day out on the firing range where we pulled targets up and waited for the guys to fire. Then we pulled the targets down and marked their shots either in red or black, then we pulled the targets back up. We had to do this over and over again. Also, it was a five-mile march back in for lunch then another five miles back to the range and five miles back home. So we did another twenty miles.

Finally we got to rest because we were around there three or four more days before we left. At the end of training I was awarded a certificate of proficiency in the use of an M1 rifle as a "sharpshooter". This was as a result of my rifle range performance and overall marksmanship evaluations.

We had no idea what was next or where we were going, and we got two weeks leave before we were to ship out. I went home to visit Mary, Viola and my Mom and Dad. I pretty much stayed around the house most of the time, just visiting and talking because I knew I was headed overseas. Mary knew where I was going but I didn't tell Mom or Dad. Mom was a big worrier, and I just couldn't bring myself to tell her the news. Deep down she probably had a good idea.

During the entire two weeks, I just wanted to stay home wrapped up in Mary's arms. One time we managed to take a stroll in Shelby Park, where we had gone on our first date.

At the end of the two weeks, Mom, Dad and Mary drove me to the train depot in Nashville. That was the saddest day of my life. It was very depressing because I was leaving Mary, and I hadn't told Mom and Dad were I was going. I caught a train back to Fort Leonard Wood and was running late getting back to the fort because of some delays in the trains. If I waited to report in at the fort, I would have been late and considered AWOL. During the war the Army had a transportation office at every train station, so I reported in at the transportation office to keep from being classified as AWOL.

When I arrived, I began packing and getting ready to go to an unknown destination. I wrote Mary a letter the night before we left.

The next day we caught a troop train headed for a Pennsylvania staging center. And, of course, I volunteered to guard the mess car. From Pennsylvania we shipped to a replacement center in New Jersey; I got a pass to go into New York. I was excited about seeing New York for the first time and called Mary from a pay station.

"Hey, Hon. I miss you already and I just got here. But guess what."

"I miss you too. When are you coming home?" There was a moment of silence and then she said, "I know you don't know. I was just trying to be funny. Do you promise to be good?"

"Yes, I promise, sugar babe and I'll write whenever I can. And I will come home!"

"Calvin, I got a parking ticket yesterday."

"Well, just go take care of it."

"It's a two dollar fine and I don't want to give them that much money."

"Well Honey Babe, if you don't pay it, then they'll suspend your licenses and you won't be able to drive."

Mary said, "I'll just park the car. I don't want to drive anyway. Where are you?"

"I'm in New Jersey somewhere near New Y..." And about that time the phone went dead. I've always believed that someone was listening and cut us off. I believe they were monitoring all calls for security reasons. Everything about our destination was very secretive and all I knew was that I had a job to do.

I just wanted to get on with it, get it done and get back home.

Wed. night

Hello hon.

How is my sweet little
wife tonight? fine I hope, hon
I sure am lonesome for you hon.

Hon it was mighty hard
to leave you hon but it had
to be done or I wouldn't of done
it for nothing in the world hon.

Hon we have been busy
all day and still busy tonight
getting every thing ready to ship
out hon. hon did you get your
cards? we got payed today I
drawed $16.50. well hon I think
we leave tomorrow if we don't
I know we leave by Sat. hon
Fuqua is still here. hon no
body stayed except 1-C or
limited service so I didn't

miss any thing did I hon.
Hon I just did git back in
time I just gave them 8 minutes
hon. Hon I sure did enjoy my
self while I was in but I could
of enjoyed it more if I hodnt
seen any body but you hon
I love you hon ond always will
you are strickly mine aint you
hon? Hon I couldnt hardly go
to sleep last night for thinking
about you hon. maby it wont
be long till we con be together
again hon I sure hope not hon
        Hon if you wont to drive
the car go out ond git it hon
ond if you dont drive it give the
gas stamp to dad if you dont
use them hon ond when that back

runs out get a new one hon
he cause you might know need
it. I love you hon do
you still love me hon? well
hon I have got to get my
things fixed up we have a
slow down inspections in the
morning. hon I will write you
some more if I have time to
night. I love you hon.
love for ever & ever & ever hon
        Calvin.

P.S. hon them sandwiches and things
there was good I didn't spend
but 18¢ all the way up here and
that was for a pack of cig. oh yes
I had to by my bus ticket from
new Bing that was 67¢.
            good night hon.

In front of mess hall

Other pictures taken during basic training

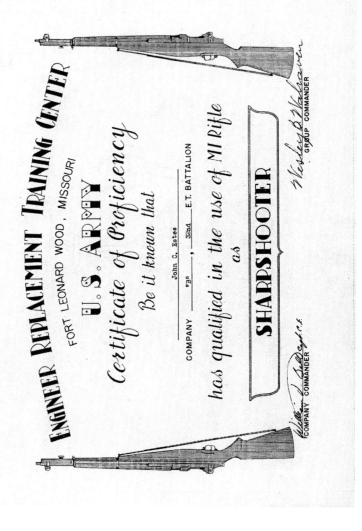

ENGINEER REPLACEMENT TRAINING CENTER

FORT LEONARD WOOD, MISSOURI

U. S. ARMY

Certificate of Proficiency

Be it known that

John C. Estes

COMPANY ___ "B" ___, 32nd ___ E.T. BATTALION

has qualified in the use of M1 Rifle

as

SHARPSHOOTER

COMPANY COMMANDER

GROUP COMMANDER

Chapter 3 - Crossing

Rangitiki (as a cruise ship)

A couple of days before we were to ship out the Army issued us some mosquito netting and bug spray. We were pissed off because we wanted to go to Europe but now believed we were headed for the Pacific. We didn't want to go there because it was hot. Then the night before we were to ship out they took back the mosquito stuff and issued us a kit that would be good for Europe.

Most of my buddies from basic training were on this ship, and none of us had any idea of exactly where we were going in Europe. Years later I heard that it was the biggest convoy of ships to ever cross the Atlantic. Early in April 1944, I boarded a ship in New York Harbor called Rangitiki, a Norwegian motorship originally built to carry cruise passengers. It was converted to a troop transport ship in 1940 and used for that purpose for the remainder of the war. In this convoy the Rangitiki was known as the Commodore's boat because the fleet commander was aboard. There were also some of my buddies from training among the twenty two hundred troops on the same ship. I noticed that there were also some stow away passengers who were unaccounted for on the ship's logs. Apparently, living on the ship was about a dozen English sparrows. I saw the sparrows flying around the ship and in and out of ledges.

Once we were on board, we were assigned hammocks. My hammock was deep down in the hull about one third back from the bow of the ship. The hull was completely open except for some support poles and my hammock was located very close to one of those poles. For some reason I was concerned that if my hammock rocked, I might hit that pole. I put both my fists right smack dab in the middle of the canvas and gave the hammock a push as hard as I could to stretch it out as far as it would go. Then I swung the hammock towards the pole and it didn't touch the pole. I felt comfortable that there was no danger in hitting the pole during the night while I slept. With only the hammocks and poles for decorations, the area was pretty drab. I didn't see any nice passenger cabins but there could have been some in the officers' quarters. I wasn't allowed in that area. Once everybody was settled in we pulled out of port.

We didn't head straight for Europe as we had expected. We detoured to meet up with other convoys along the way. The entire trip took twenty-two days, and a lot of things happened during the extra long cruise crossing the North Atlantic. During the trip only a few of us were assigned jobs, and the rest just had to kill time the best way they could. If you weren't assigned a job, there was really nothing for you to do but walk or lie around or play cards. It was really boring and I was glad to have an assignment. I was four hours on duty and four hours off. That really broke up the monotony for me.

The Navy didn't have enough sailors on board to man the guns. I believe they picked me as one of the turret gunners because of my training record and sharpshooter status. I was assigned to a station at a twenty-millimeter gun that was located way up high and pretty close to the crow's nest

.

Rangitiki painted battleship gray
and used as a troop transport ship

I was instructed to scan the waters and watch for submarines in a certain area around the ship. The German U-boats, which were small submarines, were said to be a constant problem. I had to be on the lookout for the scope of a U-boat to come up out of the water. My orders were to cut down on that scope if I saw one above the surface. I was to bury it so the sons of bitches couldn't see. There was a gunnery officer up in the bridge that was calling the shots; we had to wear our headphones all the time while manning the guns.

During gunner training they didn't explain much about the guns and only went in to detail about the sights on the guns. That seemed to be what they thought was the most important thing for a quick gunnery lesson. We were only a couple of days out when we started gunnery practice. We were told to man our stations and wait for orders from the

34

gunnery officer. I climbed the long ladder up to my gun placement area and put on my headphones. I didn't have any idea of how to shoot the thing, and before I fired my first shot I wondered what the bar rail was for that ran all the way around the gun. The railing was one of the things that the gunnery officer didn't explain, and I didn't ask him. So they throw up these forty-millimeter ack-ack (antiaircraft artillery) buffers as targets. The ack-ack's original purpose was to shoot down enemy aircraft. When its shell burst, it threw out shrapnel and a lot of smoke and was powerful enough to knock a plane out of the sky. For target practice when the shell burst up in the sky we were suppose to fire at the burst of smoke.

I was on turret number five and waiting for my instructions from the gunnery officer. I could hear the officer shouting orders to the other gun stations. I was nervous, as I got ready. I strapped myself in, stepped up to the shoulder support and put my thumb on the butterfly, which was the trigger, and was standing flat-footed behind the gun anxiously waiting to fire. Then through the headphones I heard him say, "Turret number five put me three rounds through it."

I fired immediately and the force of the gun was so hard it threw me backwards and up against the rail. The rail stopped me from falling out of the station. But the force jarred my helmet plum off and the helmet fell all the way back down on deck. I felt like an idiot as people on the deck were looking up to see if I was okay. Once they realized I was okay, they got a big laugh out of it.

I thought to myself, "Where in the hell did I shoot?" I couldn't tell because the force shook me so bad that I closed my eyes. When I opened my eyes I had temporally lost sight of the targets.

I said to the gunnery officer, "Hey, something's wrong up here! I almost fell out of this thing."

"Well, are you strapped in?"

35

"Yes, I'm strapped in!"

The gunnery officer didn't know what to say. Then I figured out that I was standing flat-footed and should have been leaning into the railing to brace myself.

So when he came around to me again, he said, "Number five to fire."

I stepped up on that rail and leaned back in to that thing and when I fired I could see I hit my target. That made me feel real good, and I was relieved.

Shortly after that they had planes fly by pulling targets and they wanted us to fire at the targets. The targets were kind of long and being pulled behind the planes. They sure did trust us not to miss and hit the planes. So the gunnery officer explained what to do next. He told me what range the planes were and where to set the sights. I shouted to the gunnery officer, "If I fire now, I'm going to shoot the plane down!" I was getting nervous again.

He asked, "You got the sights set the way I told you?"

"Yes sir!"

"So fire!"

I had to totally trust him as to where the sights were set and I fired and hit the target.

Being way up high like I was and close to the crow's nest I could look down to the deck and see just about everything that was going on. There was this pretty good size gun with maybe a five or six inch cannon and it was right on the stern of the ship. One of my buddies was operating it, and I could hear the gunnery officer talking to him. I imagined that my buddy had received just as little instruction as I had received; the way he had it pointed didn't look right to me. So I got all excited, again. I said to my ammo guy, "He's goin'a shoot the front of the other ship plum off!" Well, anyway, I held my breath as the gunnery officer gave the order to fire. When the soldier fired it hit the water about half way between the ship behind us and our ship, and then exploded. Thank goodness everything

36

was okay; I thought for sure that it was going to blow the bow of the other ship plum out. We practiced firing at the targets several times and it went very well the rest of the day and the gunnery officer was pleased.

During times when we weren't practicing and I was on duty manning my station, it was a very peaceful time just sitting there and looking out over the ocean. I was so high up that I could see something off in the distance that looked like a dark stream out in the middle of the ocean that ran as far as the eye could see in both directions from horizon to horizon. At one point dolphins were swimming and jumping in the water along this dark stream. It seemed pleasant and serene, but fascinating at the same time. The gunnery officer said, "That's the Gulf Stream and whatever those dolphins are after doesn't stand a chance."

During times when I was off duty, of course, I was playing poker and the twelve dollars I had in my pocket didn't last very long. Red, the gambler from Little Rock that I met in basic training happened to be on the same ship. He was always kind of watching but not playing. One day I was complaining to him about being broke, he said, "Well Johnny, take this five dollars and go out on deck and start a card game. Just get it going. I want to watch."

I didn't ask any questions and was excited about getting the five bucks to wager. I did just as he asked. I went out on deck, got a card game going, and lost all the money he gave me. The next day we did the same thing. He gave me money. I started another game and he'd watch. Most of the time I would lose the money.

Sounding kind of frustrated he said, "Out of twenty-two hundred people on this boat there's bound to be another card shark besides me. I'm trying to spot him. That's the guy I want to play. I don't want to take the regular GI's money." Finally, I knew what he was up to but didn't know what to look for so I couldn't help him spot the guy.

Eventually, he found the guy he was looking for. "That guy sitting right over there is the guy I want to play." As he pointed him out he continued to say, "So Johnny, tomorrow get in the same game with that guy. When I get in the game, you bet with me. I'll get my money back that you lost and all of yours, too." The other card shark had been taking the regular GI's money and Red wanted to take it from him.

The next day I got in on the card game, and then he joined. That day I won my money back and a little bit more. All the other guys in the game lost their money and the only two left in the game were ole Red and the other card shark. They were buttin' heads and Red finally broke him. During the rest of the trip I was only able to play from time to time because I was pulling duty. But ole Red played all the time because he didn't have an assignment. Also, sometimes when I was able to join in, I couldn't because they were betting too high. Afterwards, Red had quite a bit of money on him. By the end of the trip it seemed like he had all the money on the ship except for some that I had, which wasn't much.

We went through some pretty rough seas. We'd hit storms, real bad storms. I'd say that at least half of the guys were getting seasick during these storms that lasted four days and five nights. But it didn't bother me.

It was so rough we couldn't do any target practice. We were lucky enough to even be able to get up and down the ladder getting to our guns. I would try to climb up that ladder and the ship would roll to the right and then set back up and then roll over to the left. When the ship rolled way to the left or right, my gun station and the ladder going up would be out over the water instead of above the ship. One time it really rolled way left and my feet slipped off the ladder. I was just hanging there trying to get my heels to catch onto the ladder. I thought I was going to be tossed off the ship. I finally made it to the gun placement. The guy I

38

was relieving was so scared he wouldn't even try to go down. He slept in the gun turret under the gun canvas during my entire shift.

The wind was so bad it was blowing waves way up high and plum up into my gun turret. The water that was hitting my face tasted salty; I knew it was seawater. I thought about the sparrows and figured that they were probably done for and would be gone when the storm was over.

Then the next morning after this real rough night, I looked out at the tankers in the convoy and they were going plum under water. Everything looked gray; the sky, the ships, and the sea. I got my wish I made that day during my thirty day leave when Mary and I went to the Knickerbocker Theater. I had wished that I could see a terrific storm if I had to cross the Atlantic. When I looked out over the convoy, all I could see was the dog gone pilothouses. The sea was that rough. Each tanker was carrying about six planes on its top deck. I asked the gunnery officer through the headphones, "How in the cat hair were those planes going to be worth a darn with all that salt water on them?"

"Well they're covered with cosmoline. They're sort of waterproofed by being coated with a very heavy grease type compound and fixed ready to ship like that. If it gets any rougher, they're going to have to cut the planes loose."

"How in the devil are they going to get out there to cut the planes loose?"

"They'll cut them loose from the inside".

So after the second night of real rough seas and when it became day light, there were no planes on the tankers. They had cut them loose. They just dumped all the planes into the ocean.

During this rough weather you had to be able to skate if you went to the restroom. Vomit was just spilled all over the place from the garbage cans. The cans had been sitting in a round cut out like thing and all of them had jumped plum out of their places and spilled out all over the floor. Because of all the seasick guys throwing up in the cans, they were probably pretty full before they turned over. The cans were rolling all over the place, and it was a big place. Fortunately, I wasn't bothered with seasickness, but I really didn't enjoy the skating.

When I first got on the ship, I went to the restroom, and I sat down on the commode and there was an iron rail running all the way around the commode area. I wondered what that thing was for, but after we hit that storm I found out fast enough! During the storm I was sitting on the pot and the ship would roll so far to the side that I'd have to hold on to that rail to keep from falling off! The water would spill out of the commode along with whatever else might be in there. It was a rough ride.

During my first break in the midst of this rough weather, I crawled in my hammock to catch some sleep. The hammock was swinging from side to side and my butt hit that pole. I had to crawl back out of the hammock and make an adjustment.

The storm lasted four days and five nights. When the storm was over, I was surprised to see the sparrows were still there. The remainder of the trip was good for gambling and stuff like that except during the time we had an alert.

The alarms went beep, beep, beep, beep and they announced to all the gunners that we were under a submarine attack. There were two destroyers that were leading the way and they wheeled around and went back between us. Not very far back they started circling and throwing depth charges. Of course, me being way up there next to the crow's nest, I had a good view of what was going on. When the alert was over they announced that they had got the sub or knocked it out, but I didn't see anything. All I saw was the depth charges being thrown. I didn't see anything coming up like a damaged U-boat because we were so far away. During this alert the whole convoy had sped up because I could feel the vibrations from the ship as it increased its speed. You could tell they were throwing on the coal, so to speak.

Then shortly after that we got an alert that airplanes were approaching. They just said airplanes approaching from a certain direction and for us to be on the ball and not to fire until called on to fire. It wound up to be our own people that were ferrying planes across. Of course, we had the beam on them. We could have knocked them down if we wanted to because they were flying very low to avoid radar detection. The gunnery officer said they should have notified us that they were going to fly over our convoy, but they didn't. Nobody fired on them. The gunnery officer called out over the speakers that they were friendly planes.

The nights out at sea were so dark especially when the sky was cloudy. It was so dark that we had ropes out on deck to follow to get from one place to another. The ropes were marked with gun numbers. So I had to follow number five to get to my station. I mean you couldn't see anything even if it was right in front of your face. One night I was following the rope to get to my specified gun area and somebody had gotten on my rope coming the other way and we ran head on into each other and our teeth hit. I was afraid I had cracked my tooth we hit so hard. I never did know who he was or see him or nothing and we didn't say anything to each other as we continued down the rope in opposite directions.

Days passed and then finally we landed in Ireland, but weren't allowed to get off the ship. We stayed there for one night and then went over to England.

Chapter 4 - Toughening Up

We landed in Liverpool, England. I'll never forget it as long as I live. There was a band welcoming us into England, and they were playing the Beer Barrel Polka.

For miles around, you'll hear them sing
Roll out the barrel we'll have a barrel of fun
Roll out the barrel we've got the blues on the run
Zing Boom Terrara
Join in a glass of good cheer
Now it's time to roll the barrel for the gang's all here.

I didn't know at the time, but that music was a hint of what was to come. There was a German brewery in my future.

After we were settled in, Red asked me to help him send some money home. A GI was limited to a hundred-dollar money order. All he could send to his family was one hundred dollars, so I sent some money back to his family also.

While in England they about starved us to death. We were eating stew just about every day. I got my first experience with the Red Cross overseas. If it hadn't been for them, we would have gone hungrier than we did. However, I was really surprised that they made us pay for everything we got considering the amount of money being donated back in the states.

Well, every now and then we had to pull KP duty down at the Officers' Mess Hall; I knew that they were eating pretty good while we were starving. I got peeved off about it and went down to the Officers' Quarters and invited the Colonel up to eat supper with us. I had caught him just as he was about to sit down to eat. He acted disturbed when I asked him to eat with me. He asked, "Why?"

"I just want you to come up to eat. I want you to see what we eat." I was insisting as much as I could without stepping out of line.

I guess he could tell I was upset and determined when he said, "Okay, I will."

Because it took some time to convince him to come we were late getting up to the mess hall and they didn't have any stew at all left for us. As he shook his head he said, "I see your problem."

The Colonel immediately investigated the problem and found out that administration didn't even know that we were there, and so they weren't issuing enough rations. Our records were still back in the United States. We could have gone AWOL and they wouldn't have missed us. Also, because our records hadn't arrived neither had the mail and I sure was missing Mary a bunch and needed to hear from her.

While we were waiting in England for the records to get straightened out we were doing things like "close order" drilling, march left flank, march right flank, rear flank and all that stuff. We would work on what was called an assault course. It was approximately a two hundred-yard obstacle race course with rifle and pack with a time limit of about four minutes. We received briefings on German uniform and allied uniform recognition. We did some live firing on the range and were getting familiar with the equipment.

They finally got the records straight and after about three weeks in England I went to a replacement depot and was assigned to the 49th Combat Engineer Group that was a part of B Company in the VII Corp., 3rd Div., 1st Army. The units were being built up to combat strength. A unit is built up ten percent over normal strength before it goes into combat for obvious reasons.

The 49th was a battalion of approximately two thousand guys from various places all over the country. My squad sergeant was Harry Morrison, a lumberjack from West

Virginia, who was as strong as an ox. He seemed very particular about how things should be packed and would inspect everything several times. It seemed that something was always out of place and it was hard to meet up to his standards when it came to packing. Half the time he would just pack it himself. His reasoning was that he wanted us to be able to find anything we needed in the dark. In the field of combat you may not have any lights period, or it may be dangerous to turn a light on.

Then there was Corporal D. Varey from New Jersey. He spoke with that typical New Jersey accent and was always making fun of my southern slang.

I really hit it off with a fellow by the name of Donald Sneed, but we called him Junior and he was from New Orleans and small in stature, just a little o'bitty dried up looking guy.

Then there was Charles Gucciardo, from New York. He was Italian and ran his mouth a lot, and for some reason I don't like people that yak, yak, yak all the time.

Also in my outfit was Marcus Hook from New Jersey, a real quiet kind of guy who had a camera and was taking a lot of pictures.

There was Fisher, a neat and clean type guy who carried with him a pair of hair clippers and was always grooming himself, and Mayo from Kentucky, who always acted like he knew more than the rest of us. Others were Thomas Mohan from Missouri, C.F. Mergenthaler from Delaware, a fellow by the name of Abshire and D. J. Persinger, the squad truck driver from West Virginia. There were a few others, but I can't remember their names.

When I joined up with the 49th   somewhere close to Southampton, England we started the toughening up phase while waiting for our orders and getting ready for an invasion. They just called the whole battalion together and we started marching and marching and marching. They didn't tell us anything about where we were headed.

44

Everything was top secret. We just somehow knew that an invasion was coming soon.

They issued us extra equipment that we were going to have to use. They also gave us impregnated clothing to wear and gas masks in case the Germans threw gas or engaged in chemical warfare.

We did cross country marches to build our physical strength. They called it a toughening up course. We just took off in one direction and went over hills and crossed rivers on foot as if in a cross-country race.

While doing this we would end up sleeping or camping in the field, and England had these "watchers" that kept an eye on all government troops. Of course, they didn't tell us about how strict they really were. The first night we were on a bivouac. It was a stop for the night. I got out my little pup tent, and I needed a ridgepole for my tent. I saw a little bush in a sinkhole area in this field where we were camping. I cut off a piece of the bush that was just the right length, bent it over and used it for my ridgepole. That ridgepole cost the U.S. Government fifty bucks because this English "watcher" was following right behind us and writing up the damage we had done. The government had to pay for it and I did it twice before they caught me. The B Company commander, Captain Hahn, really chewed everyone's butt out.

He said, "You're not suppose to damage any trees, bushes or anything because England is really short on trees and foliage. Any damage you do will have to be paid for by our government." So I let Captain Hahn know what I had done. Come to find out he was just as surprised as I was about how strict they were.

He said to me, "Don't do that anymore and don't cut anything, period." If you could have seen the area you would understand. Even if a limb were blown out of a tree the civilians would pick it up, bundle it, and carry it with them. There wasn't any debris in the area. Everything was used. It was burned for heating or for cooking.

After all the special training I had received and then going through the toughening up phase, I felt like I was top dog or the best damn soldier in the world. I thought that nobody could beat me. Looking back I realized that it was some kind of brain washing that was given to the GI to get him ready for battle. Colonel Gallagher was always saying that war was like a football game. I was motivated and ready to get into the game and kill and destroy.

Chapter 5 - D-Day, Organized Confusion

We went to a staging area near the port of Southampton, England. They didn't tell us anything about what was planned. But we knew this must be it because they served us a meal that wouldn't quit. They fed us real good and we had music and all that kind of stuff. Then they issued us live ammo. That was a dead giveaway. We were ready to go and boarded the ship on June 4th of 1944 and left out of Southampton. The first wave loaded directly on to the LST's, and I got on to a big ship. There were thousands of the LST's (Landing Ship Tanks), each capable of transporting some eighteen thirty-ton tanks or twenty-seven three-ton Lorries and eight jeeps with up to one hundred seventy seven troops. I later found out that in addition to the thousands of LST's, there were nine battleships, twenty-three cruisers, one hundred and four destroyers and thousands more crafts and barges of all sizes carrying supplies and equipment.

A major storm came up, so we sat in the channel and waited for the weather to subside. The invasion was delayed twenty-four hours because of the storm. We had to just sit there and wait which gave us too much time to think about the situation and try to guess what was in store. After all the training and preparation the time had come, but we were not sure what to expect. We were headed into an unknown situation, and everyone was very subdued. There wasn't much talking at all. Except one of my buddies sitting next to me asked, "Johnny, if I get scared and start running, will you shoot me?"

I said, "Yea, I'll shoot you."

"You will?"

"You can count on it." I just kind of looked at him and didn't say anything else. I didn't feel much like talking. I closed my eyes and began to pray to myself something like this,

Dear Lord, Help me be a good soldier,
To serve my country,
not let my buddies down
and to make it home safely.
But Lord, if I must die
Then Lord, please make it quick. Amen

I realized that we were headed into combat and knew that the 101st airborne had already landed before daylight and I was hoping they were accomplishing their mission. Whatever in the hell that was! I was mostly very nervous as I sat quietly deep down in the hull of this ship. I couldn't see anything that was happening outside.

It was almost dead silent except for the humming of the engines. Then all of a sudden I heard planes flying over our ship where I assumed they were headed to the beaches. I imagined that the planes were over the beaches when they started dropping bombs. The noise from the exploding bombs was almost constant. At about the same time I could tell there was a big battleship nearby and just ahead of us. It was sitting out in the channel when it started launching those big shells inland. We could hear the explosions off in the distance. They shouted, "Let's go! Let's go!"

As my heart was pounding over every inch of my body, we charged up the hole. When I stuck my head in the early morning air, I could smell gunpowder mixed with sea air and could see our ship passing the battleships. The one closest by was the USS Texas. The noise from the big ship guns was now coming from behind us and over our heads. We anchored a little past the battleships and closer to shore. In the midst of all the noise, I had to transfer from the ship I was on to an LST by going over the side of the ship climbing down a net and into the LST.

Once we were loaded the LST started taking us into shore as the big shells from all the ships in the channel flew over our heads. As we approached the beachhead, boom! The Germans fired eighty-eights in on us. The shells were flying everywhere. My natural instinct was to pull back because it was heating up, but there was no place to go as I headed straight into the fire. I was real scared but had no possible retreat. There was nothing I could do but anticipate what lay ahead as I watched the shores of France grow larger and larger.

I grew more afraid as I watched the bows of other LST's being hit with those German fired eighty-eight shells and there were explosions all around us. Then an eighty-eight came in, and we took a direct hit on the bow of our landing craft just at the water line. Water started leaking in so we turned around and as the LST was starting to sink another LST picked us up, but it couldn't take us on into shore because some of the guys had lost their equipment. I was actually relieved as we headed back to the USS Texas. We climbed up a net to reach the deck of the ship. Once on the battleship more equipment was issued to those that needed it. While we were waiting to go an eighty-eight came in and hit directly into a gun pit. I imagined that the gunmen in the pit were killed, but I don't know for sure. Only a few minutes had passed by when we climbed back down in to an LST and headed back to the beachhead again.

Fear began to mount once again because it was the same thing as before with eighty-eights hitting all around us, but this time we hit the sand. I knew that the only possible way I could survive was to jump in the water and run ashore and into the fire.

The code name was UTAH Beach where Brigadier General Theodore Roosevelt landed along with twenty three thousand men of the First Army. As our boat finally made it to shore, we had to move or jump over dead soldiers to get inland. Everybody was just firing everywhere and at anything that moved. We were running, jumping, crawling and looking for cover. Our orders were to infiltrate and get inland just as fast as we could. It was just organized confusion there for a while. It seemed like we were almost shooting at each other.

The beach was kind of flat in the area where we were and the high tide or the debris line looked like it was maybe eighteen to twenty feet up on the beach. There were no trees close to or behind the beach, but I believe there were some palm trees that had fallen down for some reason and had drifted up on the beach and laying along the debris line.

I personally was confused and scared and found myself lying behind a fallen palm tree. I was firing my gun at anything that moved when one of my buddies, named Mayo, crawled up beside me. While we were firing together from a prone position he asked, "John, are you scared?"

"If you stuck that rifle barrel up my butt, I'd clip it off just like that." And I snapped my fingers.

After we fired a few more rounds he said, "I just wondered if I was the only one scared."

"Listen, them guys shootin' at us are just as scared as we are. Don't you think they ain't."

We didn't stay there for very long. We jumped up and headed further inland. By this time the channel was full of ships and all of them were firing inland. The sky was loaded with planes that were dropping bombs. This went on all day long and by the time dark came around I was exhausted and had found myself behind a little ole earthen bank at the edge of a wooded area. I kind of just laid down and was watching the show. Even though it was late at night there was so much light in the sky from the artillery going off and from the planes dropping flares that I could have read a newspaper, if I'd had one. But I was so pooped out that I fell asleep right in the middle of all the noise and probably slept there for two or three hours.

I later found out that out of twenty three thousand men coming ashore we only lost a hundred and ninety seven. That wasn't too bad, but it was a lot worse over on OMAHA Beach. They had to climb some tall cliffs and in doing so thousands of our boys were lost. I think it was a stupid place to land soldiers.

When I woke up we were getting some pretty direct hits from the enemy. As the sun started to rise we could see that there was a small town nearby. I think the name of the town was St. Mere-Eglise. One of the artillery observers was near me, and we could see a church steeple in the town. He was trying to figure out where the German observers were located so he could take them out and stop the direct hits. We were looking up over the bank and that's the only place they could have been was in the steeple.

He said, "That's where they've got to be." So he called for artillery from a ship in the channel to zero in on the church steeple. Our artillery made a direct hit and cut the steeple off. Then the direct hits on us ceased. So they were definitely in the steeple.

All during the night and next morning equipment kept rolling ashore. There were lots of vehicles: tanks, scout cars, big trucks and half-tracks along with extra small arms, ammo and supplies coming in and being off loaded from boats that would bring them almost to shore. The land type vehicles were rigged so they could run under water; they had the intake and exhaust sticking up just like a snorkel. The boats would bring them as close as possible to the shore then the front gate on the boat would drop and the vehicles would roll off and go underwater. Then you could see them come out of the water and on to the beach. The engines had been cosmolined. Coated with the same heavy grease that was used on the planes to waterproof the engines so they would work underwater as well. Later on I heard that they had built these concrete floating docks where the ships could anchor and then unload supplies. I never did get to see those floating concrete docks.

After two or three days we were still down on the beach and hadn't gotten inland very far. I had lost track of time and didn't know what day it was and didn't care, really. Some German machine guns had pinned us down. Three of us were ordered to go after the machine gun. We were slipping up on the machine gunner and trying to knock it out. When I looked down and behind me here come two sailors walking along the beach in their white sailor uniforms. They were just kind of strolling along on a beach road.

I shouted, "Go back! Go back!" The others were hollering at them too. They didn't pay any attention to us.

"We're looking for souvenirs," they shouted. About that time the German machine gun opened up on us, again. And of course, we were down behind a rocky area and hidden but the sailors were out in the open. You should have seen those sailors run. Both of those sailors reached up at the same time and grabbed their caps and really took off back to their boat. Evidently, they had come on shore bringing in supplies and stuff and decided to go sightseeing in the middle of all the shooting. Artillery was still being fired inland from the battleships. That was a dumb thing for them sailors to do. I don't know if they made it back to their boat or not.

During this invasion the allies had brought in a bunch of French-Moroccans to help us in the war. The way I understood it there was about a battalion of them or approximately two thousand French soldiers. Of course, because we were in France they wanted to take part in some way. But when they were turned loose, they scattered to the four winds. They were all over the place, and no one had any control over them. At least they had on their uniforms and we knew who they were so we didn't try to shoot them.

Mayo and I were still lying there and pinned down by this machine gun when two of these Moroccans came crawling around from our left. We couldn't understand a word they were saying. They started motioning that they were going to go get 'em.

"No! You better stay down." They couldn't understand us either.

It was broad daylight, and the Frenchmen got up and went walking off in the direction of the machine gun fire.

"Well, that's the last we'll see of those dudes." We said to each other and shook our heads with disbelief.

But shortly after that the machine gun didn't fire no more. We decided to go check it out and got up and headed towards where the firing had previously been coming from. Well here came the Moroccans, and they had two German left ears. They had cut the left ears off to prove to us that they had gotten the German machine gunners.

The German Army fought really hard and stalled us out for two or three days. At that time they gave us orders not to wear our leggings but to wear our regular combat boots, especially at night while we were asleep. Come to find out the French Moroccans would crawl around at night and feel our feet while we were asleep and if someone had on a slick boot, they would knife him. All of the Germans wore boots that were slick and didn't have laces like the regular GI boot. So they asked us to sleep with our boots on so they would know who we were.

In training, I'll call it brain washing, we were convinced to believe that we were the best damn soldiers in the world. We were taught to "kill and destroy". But when you actually get into a battle you find out quickly that there's two sides to the whole thing. The Germans had some good soldiers too. I felt this because I saw a bunch of dead GI's laying all over the place and they were constantly pinning us down to where we couldn't move or we'd be dead. I drew the conclusion that they were pretty good soldiers and

53

I found out that they were very disciplined. I realized that the other side's soldiers were just as good as I was and just as vulnerable.

The German eighty-eights were their number one artillery weapon. They could pinpoint a target anywhere they wanted too. Also, they had mortar crews consisting of three people that were very efficient.

We finally got our first little break at Normandy. We settled down and were going to rest a day or so. Everybody started pulling out little gas stoves to make coffee and it sure smelled good even though it was powdered coffee. This was the first time I'd ever seen powdered coffee. That morning I saw a cow out in the field so I cut down on that cow. I killed a cow. We went out and skinned it and got some meat. I said to Burbee our mess sergeant, "How about cooking us some steaks this evening?"

"I'll be glad to do it." He said. About the time we got the cow halfway dressed, they called my outfit back up on the line. They needed us up there quick and it wasn't very far. It was just about throwing distance, so to speak, from where I had shot the cow. We went back up and there was a little ole creek there. I called it a creek because the rivers back home in Tennessee are mighty rivers. I think most of the people in my outfit called this little ole creek a river. The Germans had blown the bridge out that crossed the creek. Our tanks couldn't get across so we had to put up a pontoon bridge.

Of course, we were on the low side of the creek and the town was sitting up on the hill or on high ground. The Germans were sitting up there sniping at us. They were about five hundred yards away and up in the buildings in the town. They had a clear view of us especially when we got over on the right side of the bridge. When they'd fire, I'd hear something go by my ear, ssssp, as it hit the dirt. They were firing at us while we were working. These buildings were pretty close to the creek bank and on the

54

high ground side. The artillery that the German's were dropping in on us was falling short and hitting the buildings. The enemy was having trouble looping the bombs over the buildings. So the bombs were hitting the buildings that were right in front of us and the Germans were knocking out some of their own soldiers. In spite of the sniper shooting and bombing, we managed to get the pontoon bridge across the creek.

While we were building the bridge, one of our new replacements was a full-blooded American Indian who we called Chief Kisto or just Chief. Ole Chief was a really good cowboy and always carried a rope with him that came in handy. He was going up and down the street near the creek and out of sight of the German snipers looking for dead German's on rooftops. He would throw his rope and lasso the corpses and pull them down. I don't know if he was doing it for fun or because he thought he was being helpful. He just liked to use that rope.

We were getting ready to pull out when here come some of our friendly planes, P47's. They came in strafing us, which is also called skip bombing. That's the first and last time I've ever seen skip bombing. What they would do was fly right down that creek. The area we were in was a river bottomland type area. They'd come in there and strafe and while they were strafing, they'd release their bombs and they would hit the ground flat. I could hear it go flop. It would hit the ground and here it would come in on us end over end or skipping along the ground. Thank goodness they missed our pontoon bridge. It didn't get hit by either the Germans or by our friendly planes.

There was a house right next to the abutment of the bridge. One of the bombs from our P47's went right through the house and leveled it when it went off. We got pinned down there and couldn't leave. The Germans really got to firing on us again. This was up in the late afternoon by the time we got pinned down.

Our planes were strafing and coming in from the left side of the bridge. Most of us went over the road and to the right side of the bridge to get away from our own planes to dodge the strafing, but on the right side of the bridge we were sitting ducks for the German gunmen. We had bullets hitting right beside us, ssssp, ssssp. So I said to myself, "Which is the safest?" And I decided to go back to the other side of the bridge. I liked those doggone planes better that those guys up there looking at me and trying to shoot me. Unless you're looking right down the engine of an airplane you're better off choosing the airplane. The fire from the plane is most of the time four to six feet apart because the four guns mounted on the plane are about four to six feet apart. I was desperately looking for cover and spotted a rock fence back a few feet from the creek.

When all of the barrage and everything really started to heat up, I wanted to get behind that rock fence for better protection. I took off running and tried to make it to the fence, but I saw that I wasn't going to be able to make it. So I dove in a bomb crater that one of our planes had just made, and there I waited it out. They gave everybody orders, "Every man for himself to get out of there!" It was a miserable, miserable feeling just lying there under fire for that long of a period. I just lay there and tried to decide, "Should I stay or should I try it? I should stay! No, I should go for it! I should go for the fence. Please God help me decide." I decided to stay and it was a good thing. I stayed huddled in the bomb crater until a little after dark.

When I came out of the bomb crater I actually walked over that rock fence. It had been turned to rubble. It's a good thing I didn't make it to the fence.

When I got out of there and back to my outpost, I asked Burbee, "Did you save me any steak?"

He said, "Yea, I saved you one piece."

The steak was burnt but I enjoyed it anyway. I was so thankful for being able to eat that steak. It didn't matter how it tasted.

Harry Morrison, the Squad Sergeant ordered, "Pack 'em up. We've got a new mission. And try to load the damn truck right this time."

Chapter 6 - Around Cherbourg

After breaking though the Germans at Normandy, we were told our mission was to get Cherbourg. It was the nearest port to our location. We sent out patrols and they came back and reported that there was a bunch of German artillery scattered all over the place. It appeared that Cherbourg was heavily guarded with a large amount of artillery.

As we were moving towards Cherbourg, we were clearing houses. We were doing our usual going from house to house and door to door making sure the area was cleared of any possible danger from the German soldiers. There were a lot of dugouts back in the banks of the roads that ran up to the houses in this one area. We thought we saw three Germans run in a house. The dugouts ran from the road and came out up into the yard. So my buddy and me ran through the yard and went up to that house quick like while the other guys covered us. When we made it to the side of the house we stopped and turned our backs against the wall to catch our breath. While leaning with my back to the wall, I lit a cigarette and took a long draw from it and was about to go in to the house. Ole Chief came walking out of the dugout. When he did I fired from the hip and missed and was about to fire a second time when I recognized him.

"Golly Chief, I liked to have got ya!"

"Johnny, you smoke too much." That was his answer. It didn't excite him a bit.

As we got closer to Cherbourg, we ran into, destroyed and captured a German artillery convoy that was also headed for Cherbourg. Horses were pulling all of the German artillery and it looked strange. The horse drawn artillery consisted of modernized weaponry being pulled along the road by horses. Our artillery killed so many horses that day that the roads were blocked and we were stalled and couldn't advance. A well-known reporter by the name of Ernie Pyle was there and took a lot of pictures of the dead horses. I remember him saying while kicking a few German boots that were lying on the ground, "Damn, what a mess." After kicking the boots around he found out that there were severed German legs still in the boots.

Horse and human flesh and bones were strewn everywhere. Ernie reported about it in the Stars and Stripes a publication that was distributed to the troops whenever they could get them to us.

Ernie Pyle said in his article published in The Stars and Stripes on Thursday, June 29, 1944, "We had caught the Germans trying to retreat down the road from Brie Quebec to Barnesville and plastered them with artillery. The devastation along that road was immense and the Germans were moving with many horse drawn vehicles, as well as trucks.

They were in two-wheeled French work carts, in fancy passenger buggies and in light wagons along the style of our own wild west covered wagons. At spots their wreckage was piled so high that traffic couldn't get through, until our own engineers dragged debris off the road.

A bulldozer methodically pushed dead horses and shattered trucks, all in the same scoopful, off the road into an orchard. The dozed driver went after his job with a grim got-to-do-it look on his face.

As the bulldozer pushed, a little bunch of French people stood looking on. Bert Brandt took pictures while standing on the hood of a command car in which we had been riding. I sat in the back seat, calling to him to hurry up and finish. Of all the war I've seen, that is the sight which has come nearest to making me sick at the stomach."

It was the combat engineer's job to clear the way but we needed heavy equipment to move the debris. While we waited for bulldozers to arrive to remove the horse corpses and other wreckage, we set up an outpost near a hedgerow that was between two fields. The first thing we did was dug ourselves a foxhole near the hedgerow. Just a little ways out in to one of these fields we dug a slit trench. A slit trench is a ditch to use as a latrine. We dug so many holes that I thought that when I got back home I'd be a foreign soil expert.

B Company, which was my company, was on the right side of the outpost and C Company was on the left. About midnight, C Company's outpost fired two machine guns. Of course, that put us on alert for the rest of the night. The next morning at daylight we came out from behind the hedgerows and went in to the open field. The grass and weeds in the field had grown up pretty high. As we were walking through the field, German gunmen started rising up all over the place. It pretty much scared my pants off, to tell you the truth, when these gunmen started rising up out of the grass with their hands up and hollering "Comrade, comrade!" This is who C Company had fired on during the night and they all had just hit the dirt and stayed low and hidden in the tall grass. We captured all of them, and believe it or not, two of their officers where both hit in the butt. We gave them first aid and sent them on the way. Well not exactly on their way, we turned them over to some MP's, who took them as prisoners.

While waiting one day I went out in the field to use the slit trench. I had my pants down and was busy doing my business when the German's started firing eighty-eights at us. A few yards in front of me an eighty-eight dug right into the ground threw up the dirt and slid straight towards me. You can imagine what kind of scrambling I was doing trying to get out of the way. Luckily, it was a dud and didn't go off. Unfortunately, I dove right into some unpleasant stuff and had to wipe it off the best way I could.

While we were waiting to move out, there were what appeared to be real wild horses running around in a field. Old Chief decided to show off his cowboy skills.

"I can catch anyone of those horses you want."

"Well, how are you going to do that?" I asked.

"I'll rope 'em."

"You can't rope those horses. They're too wild and won't even let you get close." So he went out into the field and roped one right quick like. He hemmed the horse up against the fence then ran it out from the fence and roped it with the first try.

"I'll be damned if you didn't get one."

"I can trip him if you want him tripped."

"What do you mean, trip him?"

"I'll lasso his front legs."

And I said, "So, show me." He lined the horses up against the fence again and then ran one out from the fence and with the first try he lassoes both front legs and tripped the horse. He was just that good. He had that rope with him back in Normandy and he still had it. I figured he must carry that rope with him wherever he goes.

Our mission was still to take Cherbourg and with the patrol reports of the large number of German artillery guarding the port, we were mounting our attack on the town. By the way, it was right in this area where I had my 21st birthday, June 22, 1944.

Finally, the bulldozers arrived and shoved the horses off the road and the engineers moved the debris out of the way so the tanks could move in. When we got up close we fired at the German artillery but nothing happened. They didn't fire back and come to find out all of the reports of this artillery was not exactly right. It was dummy artillery. The Germans had trimmed pine trees back in several different places and put up camouflage nets over the trimmed trees. Our patrols had to crawl around in the dark trying to see, and in total darkness they thought it was artillery. It looked just like artillery, but there wasn't any in there, period.

The city of Cherbourg is right down underneath a big bluff. The bluff backs right up over the city and we were up on top of the bluff trying to get the Germans to surrender. We had them cut off and they didn't have anywhere to go because the English Channel was behind them and we were inland and blocking their exit.

While we were trying to get them to surrender, a jeep comes buzzing up the hill. It was a German jeep and it had one of our soldiers in it. They had captured quite a few of our infantrymen. The jeep driver, a German sergeant, was flying a white flag.

"We've got several wounded and need medical supplies," said the American soldier.

"You get out of the jeep and we'll send the driver back with the supplies."

"No, I told him I'd come with him. So I'm going back. But I'll tell you this; you don't have to worry about hitting any of our guys." The German sergeant kind of hit him across the shoulder so he'd shut up.

At that time we didn't know what he meant. So we gave them the supplies and they left. We continued to fight and then we found out that there was a big cave and we were standing on top of the cave at that time. When the jeep had buzzed up where we were, all the prisoners were underneath us in that cave. I mean it was a monstrous cave.

We were working at destroying some big eighty-eight guns and other German artillery when the 29th infantry division came into the town from our right flank and took the town and set the American prisoners free from the cave.

My engineer squad started clearing buildings. We were going from house to house and door to door. There was a booby trap set on a big trophy case in one of the houses and one of our guys opened it up and was killed.

While this was going on the dumb nut that was commanding the 29th infantry battalion called formation. I don't know why he called a formation to begin with. It was stupid. In the field of combat you never group a bunch of guys together. But he called all of his infantrymen together, and they all lined up and had their formation. They bunched up right out on the main street that runs right along the water's edge. There was a whole bunch of pillboxes sticking up out of the water and all along the whole area. A pillbox is a concrete dome like thing that sticks up out of the water and has gunmen inside and under the water. These pillboxes opened up the tops and slaughtered a whole bunch of infantrymen that were right there and all lined up. Of course, we started returning fire and they buttoned them back up. Then we were stalled again.

There we were and it was the combat engineer's job to clear the pillboxes, but we didn't have any equipment to do it with; especially boats that we needed to get out to the pillboxes in the bay. So we called for a P47 bombing. P47's were dive-bombers. They would come in there and with their nose straight down and drop a bomb on the pillboxes. The dive-bombing went on for a couple of days because a small pillbox was hard to hit. We were setting up on shore and watching the action. We were kind of taking it easy, enjoying a cup of coffee and waiting for the bombers to do their job. Every time a bomber would come over and start his nose-dive at a pillbox we would bet as to whether or not he'd hit it or miss it. Anyway, I lost a few bucks, and I made a few bucks. We were enjoying it because we didn't have to get out there and do it ourselves. They finally hit most of the pillboxes, and the ones not hit surrendered and the situation turned out pretty good, except for that stupid formation.

Chapter 7 - Caen Airfield

We moved out of Cherbourg and headed straight back where we had come from. Another force went to our right to cut off the port at Le Havre, France, and we headed straight-ahead into the main force of the German army. It seemed like there were a lot of British soldiers assisting us in this area.

Our next mission was to capture an airfield so we could get our planes in the area. The airfield was near the town of Caen. We had to get that airfield for our planes because they were making bombing runs all the way from England.

It seemed that in this area of France, most of the local people that we ran into were very rural and hadn't traveled very far from home. On more than one occasion, we'd asked them for directions and they couldn't tell us how to get there even if it was only fifteen miles away because they'd never been there. They couldn't even tell our interpreter.

After we figured out which way to go to get to the airfield, Colonel Gallagher, who was in-charge of B Company, called a formation. This made a lot of us nervous after what we'd just witnessed in Cherbourg. The sergeants shouted, "B Company formation!" Everyone hustled into formation and stood at attention. Colonel Gallagher walked up and said, "Men, as you know I like to think of war as a football game and we have just won the first down. There will be many more plays to execute and as your coach, I intend to lead you to victory. I will send in the plays and it's your job to execute the plays as instructed and to gain yardage."

I didn't like that at all and neither did by buddies! After a few days in battle it was clear that there were no similarities between war and a football game. I had to bite my tongue to keep from telling him exactly what I thought.
64

That analogy made the situation seem trivial and just for sport as if we wanted to be playing for fun.

Also, Colonel Gallagher tried to act like a big brave guy and wanted to be right up at the front lines all the time. As we moved towards Caen, we ran into a small arms fight. Some of the guys got pinned down, including Colonel Gallagher, who crawled into a culvert pipe. We were close enough that we could holler at him and talk back and forth. We told him to wait until after dark before he tried to get out because the Germans would have a clear shot at him in broad daylight. Well he didn't listen because he didn't want to wait. So he shouted, "Cover me!" We started firing but it didn't do any good. The Germans mowed him down. He was killed right there. We kept fighting and finally broke through the small arms resistance because we simply outnumbered the Germans at that point.

We continued our move and we found the airfield. My buddy and me were ordered to scout the area. We were crawling up a ditch right at the edge of the airfield to get a closer look at the place and we were hoping not to be seen. We thought we might need to do some demolition or clearing, so we were trying to look at the airfield to see what we had to do, figure out what we could do and determine if the enemy was occupying the airfield.

Bushes had grown up over the ditch. We crawled right up under the bushes and down the ditch until we got as close to the fence as we could. We were almost to the fence of the airport when someone threw a German hand grenade, which we called a potato masher. It looks like a round thing with a wooden handle. When he threw the potato masher, it landed right up over our heads. In other words, someone saw us and made a good throw and it hit right up over our heads but lodged in those bushes.

We backed up in a hurry. If you've ever seen a crawdad move, that's how we looked crawling backwards as fast as we could down in the ditch and under the bushes. The potato masher was evidently a dud because it didn't go off. It just kind of hung there in the bushes. So we had to crawl back up under the bushes again with that potato masher dangling over our heads.

When we got back up to the fence, we didn't see anyone there. The only thing we could figure out was that whoever made the throw must have seen us, tossed the potato and took off running. We knew it had to be a German soldier.

After we got to the airfield we determined that we didn't have to do anything as far as demolition or clearing debris. In other words, we went in there and captured it with not a whole lot of problem. Then the Army engineers came in and repaired the field. Army engineers did mostly construction type work. So with the capture of this airfield our planes could fly shorter distances, and therefore, about five times more sorties.

We moved out of Caen, final destination Berlin.

Johnny somewhere on the road

Johnny is fourth from left with buddies.

Johnny in the far back

Johnny lying down

Johnny bending over with jackhammer

Some buddies washing clothes

Buddy posing with gun

Chapter 8 - Through France and Belgium

I can't remember how long we were in France or where exactly we crossed over into Belgium because we were going across country, down roads, any way we could to get there. The combat front line is not just a line that's drawn while you're driving out or down a road. You've got to cover the whole area. A front is fields and all. That's what they call a front. So we just moved on inland; just kept driving as far as we could each day going through France and headed straight towards Belgium. Our new Colonel, the one that took Colonel Gallagher's place, joined us somewhere in France. We really liked him a lot. He seemed like a soldier's Colonel. We were confident he would treat us with respect.

The local people had pretty much moved out of the area. As we would be moving into an area, the locals would be moving toward us trying to get out. They were trying to get away from the Germans and coming toward us because we were friendly troops. Also, they knew what was about to come off. But in doing so it sometimes caused a bad problem with them clogging up the roads. Because my job was to clear the way, I had to get rough with them sometimes to get them out of the way.

We received communications that the Germans were nearby and several of us were ordered to crawl through a field and get as close as we could to the enemy to gather information. We were crawling along on our bellies and ole Carlos, the Mexican from basic training at Fort Leonard Wood, was crawling right beside me. The field was divided with several fences. We'd crawl up to a fence and climb over it as fast as possible then start crawling again. At the second fence, Carlos and I stood up together to climb over. A German tank fired at us and I looked over at Carlos, and he was just standing there without a head. His head had been knocked completely off and his body was standing, then moments later fell to the ground. The rest of us had to retreat at that time because the Germans started firing heavily and there were explosions all around.

This was not too far from Cherbourg and into France at St. Lo. For several days in this area we'd take a little ole hill then the Germans would drive us off the next day. Then we'd take the hill again. One time at St. Lo we were having trouble and all of a sudden we saw our artillery that's behind us turn the guns around and face the other direction. I thought, "What the heck is coming off here?" We got word that the Germans had us surrounded. Shortly after that we were told that the Germans were throwing gas in their artillery and a gas alarm was sounded. I put on my gas mask, but ole Chief had lost his gas mask. He looked at me and started walking towards me.

"I ain't got no gas mask, Johnny."

"Well, you ain't getting this one."

"Then I'll go get me one of my own," and he left. We were still getting some incoming artillery fire and in about twenty or thirty minutes Chief came walking back from the way he had left. He was wearing a German gas mask.

"Where'd you get that gas mask?"

"Don't worry about it, Johnny." Come to find out the Germans had thrown some phosphorus shells and someone thought it was gas and sounded the alarm.

Chief was kind of a mysterious guy. He would disappear for days and then suddenly show back up. Captain Hahn would say, "Well, I ain't going to worry about him or get him for desertion. Just let him do his own thing."

Once again, we were digging foxholes all over the place. My foxhole was about the normal size for a foxhole, two feet deep. It's best to have your foxhole two-feet deep because concussion at that level will go over the foxhole. If it's deeper, then the concussion will swerve in to the hole and wound or kill the occupant. So two feet deep is about right or just below ground level.

I felt bad about digging holes and messing up the landscape around St. Lo because it was such a pretty area. There was a huge apple orchard there and the apples on the trees were about the size of big marbles. And all around the trees were big grassy areas and a big green hedgerow surrounded the grassy areas. But we had no choice; we had to call in the bombers to lay down a rolling barrage because we were absolutely locked down. A rolling barrage is where you start firing at a certain point and roll forward with continued firing. The planes and the artillery do the same thing.

The way it was supposed to work was the P47's or dive-bombers would lead the way in and hit the targets that had been set. Then that showed the A20 bombers where to start and then the B17's and the B24's were to come in behind the A20's. So the date and exact time to start the barrage was set, and my outfit was the one that laid the targets or set the markers for the bombers to start bombing. The targets were called bars and were color-coded and about eight feet long. We went out in to no man's land and placed the bars to show where to start bombing.

Before the rolling barrage started we moved up real close to the Germans and had all the tanks set and ready to go. The bombers were suppose to start bombing in front of us and roll towards the Germans. After we had set the markers, I had dug in behind the hedgerow and beside the apple orchard and was waiting for the bombers

I just kind of stood up beside a tank looking for the bombers and talking to the tank crew. Then something told me to sit down, just sit down! I thought to myself, "you'd better sit down, boy." We were pretty close to the German line. I sat down in my foxhole and the Germans fired a tank and if I hadn't sat down, it'd taken my head off. It went through the hedgerow cutting the bushes; it went right over my foxhole and exploded behind me. There were other people around me in their foxholes but I was in my foxhole by myself. You don't share your foxhole with anybody else. It's a private foxhole. It's not a fox den.

Left to right, back: Fisher, Gucciardo, and Sneed. Front: Johnny with rifle and Varey

After the German tank had fired and it seemed to have quieted down again, I moved back over behind the tank that was setting there ready to go. I was on the friendly side of the tank. Nobody was in a big hurry because the bombing was supposed to last eighty minutes, and then we were supposed to jump off or move forward. And then the bombers showed up. Here came the 8th Airforce. The tank commander had his field glasses out and looking up into the sky towards the bombers.

He said, "Here they come." It looked like a bunch of ants flying out of the ground. I mean it looked like there were thousands of them. And here they came; the P47's lead the way and dived bombed, hit the targets, pulled out, and went on their way. They were supposed to show up at twenty minutes after the hour and the entire barrage was suppose to last eighty minutes, eighty minutes of intense bombing.

The P47's came in and dive bombed right on the target and then went on their way and then here came the A20's.

And this tank commander said, " They've opened the bomb bay doors!" Well we could see them with our naked eyes. They were only bombing from about fifteen hundred feet.

The tank commander shouted again, "The bomb bay doors are open! Take cover! Bombs away!" Then he dove into his tank, and the tank crew started diving in as well. They gave the "every man for himself" order. Well, we had to make a run to our foxholes as the bombs were landing all around us. And the other A20's and the B17's and the B24's had started doing the same thing. Every plane was following the lead of the first plane. The bombs were going off, the dirt was flying everywhere, and I barely made it back to my foxhole. This went on for about eighty minutes, eighty minutes of pure hell as GI's were getting hit all around me.

When the barrage had stopped, I peeked out of my hole and could see some of my buddies nearby who had lost limbs, arms or legs. They were in a lot of pain and were crying out for help. Because they were hit with mortar fire I knew they would not bleed to death because the fire from the mortar had burned the flesh and cauterized the blood vessels. I was hoping they could just hold on until the medics could get to them. If they had been hit by shrapnel instead of mortar fire then the story would have been different. They would have bled to death in a matter of a few minutes.

The German's attacked immediately after the eighty minute rolling barrage. So we took off to get out of there as fast as we could. We had to leave some of the wounded

78

behind. As I came out of the hole I could see no grass in the area. There were no apples, no leaves, no nothing. The once beautiful apple trees were now charred shadows behind a thick blanket of smoke. It looked like a huge fire had come through and burned everything. Everything was black and gray.

Apple orchard after barrage and the little hill at St. Lo

Our own friendly bombers, I believe it was the 8th Air Force, killed ten thousand of our people that day including General McNair, who was way behind the front line. It was just a foul up. But they called us back up to the front line and we stayed up the biggest part of the night regrouping. The commander announced that it would be the same thing the next day at the same time. The Germans had damaged us was their reason for doing it again. We moved back up and laid the markers again and dug fresh foxholes. This time, when I saw the bombers coming, all I could do was pray that they would hit the right target. And sure enough, that time they hit it right and we got on the move and moved for quite a while.

When we jumped off most of the Germans were dead. But the few we saw still alive after the bombing where just sitting on the side of a foxhole. They were just sitting out in the open and dumb-founded like they'd been hit on the head with something. They were just bewildered because we'd jarred them up so much. It was easy for the MP's to round them up because they were in a state of shock.

We headed straight for Paris, and we were moving pretty good in the Paris area because we weren't moving through any opposition. The city of Paris wasn't messed up much. I didn't see any damage in the area we were in. When we got into Paris, we kind of by passed the main downtown area. The FFI, the underground French outfit, had already taken Paris before we even got there. So we just kind of bypassed it. I remember as we were going through there we passed by the Hall of Mirrors building at Versailles where the WWI treaty was signed in June 1919, The Treaty of Versailles. It was located out in the suburbs. As I passed by, I remember thinking that it didn't take the German's long to break every single provision of the treaty which they had promised to keep.

As we were going around Paris there was this French soldier chasing a German soldier. He was up on the roof of a big building, and he was shouting for us to shoot him.

"Shoot him! Shoot him! Shoot him!"

We were laughing at him and shouted back, "You better run and catch him, boy!" Anyway we didn't help him out.

It was just a funny thing to see. He was chasing one German, and we were looking for bigger fish to fry. I don't know if the ole boy got him or not. But the Frenchman had one of them old type guns that looked like a "Long Tom". They always say you could put a man's name and address in a Long Tom and it'd get him wherever he was. We moved around past Paris to Roissy, France. That's where we halted and regrouped.

After setting up camp and getting a good night's sleep, Captain Hahn told us that we could go into town for a little rest and relaxation if we wanted too. Four of the guys decided to go and wandered into a French bar that had a bunch of French women working in there, and it was heavily patronized by a large group of black GI's that worked on the Red Ball Express. That's the group of GI's that were truck drivers who brought us supplies up on the front line.

Evidently, the supply guys didn't like any combat GI's coming in and talking to the French women, so they started harassing the guys in my company.

I was told that as soon as they walked in to the bar, the black soldiers gave them the look over then started standing up puffing their chests out as if they were bulls protecting their herd. One of the supply guys said something like, "Hey you, these girls ain't got no interest in any tiny little cracker dick. So why don't you move on and get your drink somewhere else?"

One of my buddies probably said something like, "Ain't no damn nigger going to talk to me like that!"

As the ten to fifteen black guys started to move forward, the four white guys from my outfit wised up and left the building and came back to camp. Of course, they were looking for reinforcements, which included me.

Ten to fifteen of us drove back to the bar and as soon as we walked in a fight broke out. I mean the whole bar was one big brawl. We were fighting up on the bar; up on tables and down on the floor. After a while, we could tell we weren't making any headway, and someone shouted, "Let's get the hell out of here!" So we headed for the door as fast as we could go and made our way back to camp. Someone told Captain Hahn about what happened, so he ordered us to pack up and move out.

It was around about this time that we were getting really tired of Harry's attitude about packing the squad truck. He was real particular about how we packed our gear and stuff in the squad truck. Junior Sneed and I decided to play a joke on ole Harry. We were always playing jokes and kidding each other. It helped us make it through the day.

We decided that we'd disarm a regular hand grenade and put it back together. Then we'd start an argument when Harry got up in the truck to see that everything was just right. Somehow during the argument we'd get Harry involved and then throw the grenade up in the truck. So we planned it ahead of time. The inside of a grenade is gunpowder and we just dug it out and rinsed it out to be sure all the powder was out. Then I hung the dud hand grenade on my bandolier support. Normally we carried two or three grenades on the bandolier support. I always carried three, but I hung the dud up on the top. So we started the argument, "No, you fucking idiot. We're not supposed to put those damn duffel bags over there. You know that the damn ammo boxes go in first!"

"No, I'm sure Harry said it goes over on this side and the damn ammo boxes go on top."

"Listen asshole, if we don't get this right, it's going to be on your fucking back because I'm sick and tired of taking it in the ass for you."

After a while of this Harry finally chimed in and said, "Shut up! And get the damn stuff up there like I want it."

"But which shit goes first?"

Acting disgusted with us, Harry said, "I'll tell you which shit goes first. You guys don't hand me anything if I don't ask for it." And he jumped up in the truck.

I chimed in with him and said, "Oh, you're going to get in on the fucking argument too?"

He looked back at me and started moving things around.

I acted like I was getting real mad and said, "Uh cock face, you want to get smart with us now?"

I stormed off the truck, reached up and grabbed the dud hand grenade and said, "Here, pack this up there where you want it."

Then I pulled the pin and pitched it up in the truck. Harry went right over the front end of the truck, right over the fifty caliber guns, like a worm, close to the hood and over the winch close to the front bumper. Junior and I were the only ones that knew about the practical joke so all the rest of the guys ran to get out of the way. Of course, we started laughing and jumping around because it was real funny to us. But we liked to have got our butts whipped for doing such a thing. Luckily for us most of the guys were tired from the fight back at the bar, but everyone around was real pissed at us.

We finished loading up and moved out and drove right pass the bar where the fight had broken out. The convoy was passing by very slowly and we could hear laughter and music coming from behind the closed doors. The pinpoint jeep was in the lead followed up by four more jeeps. Each jeep had a fifty caliber machine gun mounted on top and was occupied by some of those involved in the fight. I was in my squad truck. As the convoy continued to move past, suddenly one of the guys in a jeep shouted, "Let's give them something to remember us by, boys." Then he opened up with his fifty and the other jeeps followed. All five jeeps were firing directly into the bar. They shot out all the windows, the signs and broke up the building pretty bad. I can just imagine what happened inside. Only when we were completely past the bar did the firing stop. Captain Hahn never said a word about it.

We were planning on spending Christmas around Verviers, Belgium. We kept on moving until we reached the town and then settled in to a building. A Belgium citizen approached me about buying some cigarettes. He owned the building that we were staying in which was a newspaper printing company before the war. I told him I could get him a whole case.

I got Harry Morrison and we went over to the supply guy. We told him what we were going to do to this guy because he was dealing in the black market. We took all the cigarettes out of the cartons that where in two full cases. Then we took some lumber that was two by fours and cut them into small pieces long enough to fill each carton. We sealed the cartons back and put them back into the case box and sealed the cases. Then we took the two cases to the guy. We got the money and he put them in his car and drove away.

We saw him the next day and he didn't say anything about it. He must have sold the cigarettes to someone else and didn't know at the time what we had done.

On the second night in Verviers we were called out in the middle of the night. The Germans were dropping paratroopers who we believed were on reconnaissance trying to gather information. We loaded up on trucks in the middle of the night and drove out of town. The commander tapped us on the shoulder one at a time as we drove down the road. When we got the tap we jumped out in complete darkness. We caught about eight to ten paratroopers.

I believe it was in this town in Belgium where Chief Kisto found a small white dog with light brown patches on his head. It looked like a Jack Russell Terrier and was rummaging around for food and looked lost or abandoned. So he picked the dog up and brought it along with him. He fed it and took care of it and called it Spot. Ole Spot acted like he was well trained when Chief found him. That dog would stay right with him at all times. The dog seemed like he knew exactly what Chief was saying or what he meant because he would do exactly what Chief asked him to do.

Hook and Chief and Spot

Spot would follow Chief in and out of houses and hang out with him around campfires and sleep with him in his pup tent. If ole Chief was busy and messing around the convoy, Spot would be acting like a dog by running up and down the convoy. He would sniff and smell and piss and run all over the place. After a couple of days they pulled us out of Verviers and sent us on a mission to take Aachen, Germany. When it came time to leave, Captain Hahn always shouted, "Wind 'em up". The lead truck drivers would wind the engines or crank engines and pass it on back. The troops would jump into their appropriate squad trucks. Ole Spot would always come running and jump in the same truck whether or not Chief was in there. And all the trucks looked alike except for the numbers on the side doors. Spot had a nose for Chief.

Chapter 9 - Aachen, Bath of the Gods

The rest of our journey through Belgium wasn't too bad. We went through Liege, Belgium and ran the Germans out and continued to push them back into Germany. Our next mission and number one target was to capture Aachen, Germany. We had heard that Aachen was Germany's pride and joy; it was their show town or best town and located right over the Belgium border. Aachen still has the warmest sulfur springs in central Europe and a ton of ancient history. Because it was their prize city the Germans really set up an opposition. We were among the first American forces to cross over into Germany. While going through France and Belgium we were a little more respectful of the citizen's personal property than we were when we reached Germany. The guys' morale was high-spirited, and we were glad thinking that we were one step closer to getting home as we were knocking on Germany's front door. The Germans had invited us to come calling, and we intended to make ourselves at home.

We were frog jumping and pushing through the country, and every once in a while I had to have some fun and play around by teasing someone. It kept me from going batty. Some of us were walking along a road because the convoy was moving pretty slow, and it gave us a chance to stretch our legs. However, we were being very cautious at the same time because we didn't know when we would run into German soldiers. Ole Chief was up in front of me as we walked along. I'd slip up behind him and pitch gravel or little rocks. It'd spook him as it would anybody because we were in a very intense situation and listening for any movement along the roadside.

"Stop it," He'd say.

I'd wait a few minutes, and then I'd do it again. He finally got enough of it and he turned around and walked back to me and looked me right in the eye.

"Damn it Johnny, don't do that no more!" When he did that and looked me right in the eye, I knew he meant it. So I didn't do that anymore.

When we reached the outside of the city of Aachen, we found that the city was re-enforced and heavily guarded by the Germans. So we had to stop outside of the city, and there we faced the Germans hardest fought battle to save that town.

We were held up in a little railroad station just outside of the town and I remember the World Series was on. Our radio operator had lined it up somehow or another for us to listen to the World Series. We enjoyed it so much that we stayed up all night long listening to the game. That was October of 1944. The St. Louis Cardinals, National League, was playing the St. Louis Browns, American League. The Cardinals eventually won four games to two. During the time of the 1944 World Series, we frequently used the password of "Yankees", the reigning World Champions. When a guy went out on patrol to get back into the area he had to answer the question, "Who won the World Series?" And we were to say "halt" one time. The patrol only had one chance to spit out the password, and if he didn't then our orders was to fire on him. He would have one chance to say, "Yankees". Fortunately, we didn't have to shoot anyone at this time.

We were at this little railroad station for several nights getting organized to attack Aachen. The Germans were all the time trying to fool us. They would get out in no man's land, which was in between our line and the enemy's line. They'd get close enough that we could hear them and they'd yell for help.

"I'm wounded. Somebody come help me. Please somebody come and help me."

They'd try to get us to fall for that and go out and try to help them and then get ambushed, but we were trained not to fall for this trick. Of course, if we had a buddy down we knew it, and that was a different situation. But if someone just started yelling for help that meant it was probably a set up. We could have helped a lot of German soldiers who really were injured, but we didn't dare because of all the fake attempts to lure us out into no man's land.

Night patrols were usually done in teams of two. I was in the regular rotation to do night patrols. This is where my Army Ranger training came in handy. To get ready to go we'd dress in dark clothing, wear a soft hat and boots. We would not carry anything that could possibly make a noise, not even our rifle. The only weapons that I carried were a trench knife, some bailing wire, and maybe my forty-five stuffed in my pants.

One night we quietly passed through no man's land and infiltrated behind the German line within the city of Aachen. My buddy and me snuck in to a German camp and actually stepped over German soldiers as they slept. We were moving slowly and cautiously and saw two German guards. In order to make it past the guards we had to take them out. I was to take one guard and my buddy would get the other. We had to do the job without waking the sleeping soldiers lying on the ground. I would reach the first guard before my buddy reached the second. With my trench knife in hand, I slowly moved close behind the first guard. He had no idea I was anywhere near. I was close enough to the German that I could have given myself away with a deep breath on his neck. With one quick move I reached around from his back to his face, stuck the trench knife through his right eye socket, gave the knife a quick jerk and he was gone. My left arm kept him from falling to the ground. The whole act happened in complete silence and just the way I was trained. A second later, my buddy did the same to the other guard. We were able to move around the enemy's camp, locate heavy guns, determine tank positions, estimate the number of soldiers and gather other strategic information without being detected. Then we reported back to the command post.

I went on this kind of mission several times. One time my buddy and I were in a trench near a German camp, when friendly fire started coming in on the Germans. We were close enough that the American tank shells were hitting all around us. I'm lying down in this trench and my buddy is a few feet away when a shell comes in right on us. After the smoke clears I look over at my buddy and he's been blown in half. His upper half is completely separated from his lower half, torn apart in the abdominal area, but he's still alive. I knew he wasn't going to make it and would suffer tremendously as all the blood in his body leaked out on to the ground unless I did something to help. I pulled out my forty-five and fired one time through his temple.

Mercy killings happened. Soldiers have an unspoken pledge to help each other, one way or the other.

We determined that the Germans had so many men and equipment in there that we had to level the city to capture it. The orders were given and the bombing went on for hours. After we finished our bombing runs and artillery attacks we couldn't drive through Aachen. We had to get in there with a bulldozer. As we went throughout Aachen, the carnage was so bad that we had to shove the debris and corpses out of the way to get through.

We were rolling down streets in the middle of town and clearing the way. There were dead soldiers and civilians all over the place, hanging from the tops of buildings, out of windows and lying in the streets. Clumps of human flesh were splattered on the few walls still standing. Burned out vehicles contained charred bodies and most building were turned to rubble. We didn't have the time or the manpower to separate human remains from the debris. Everything was just shoved together and to the side so we could get through. At this point, we had all become callous to death, and the thought of killing a human being meant no more than stomping the life out of a bug.

After getting through Aachen and all during the following night while we lay in our tents we could hear ole Chief moaning and groaning. When I saw him the next day I asked, "What's wrong, Chief?"

He hadn't said anything to anybody.

He said, "My head is hurting." So I looked at it and it was swollen, and I thought it had been hit with shrapnel or a bullet or something. We carried him to a field doctor. The doctor told him, "Man Chief, you've been shot."

The bullet was lodged in the left temple. And ole Chief said, "I have!" The field doctor sent him back in the core area to the hospital. They would eventually bring him back even though he was wounded because the commanders didn't want to lose those "seasoned troops" with combat experience.

After we destroyed Aachen we continued moving through Germany and were headed for the Hurtgen Forest. We were pushing through small towns and checking houses as we went. I was checking this one house and was going from room to room and opening doors to make sure no one was hiding in a closet. I got down close to the floor to look and see if there were any boots in there that someone could be standing in. I didn't see anything and had turned and started out of that room to go to the next room.

Then I heard this thump and this soldier pushed the clothes back and opened fire. Evidently, he had climbed several feet up the sides of the closet walls by pressing out with each foot on opposite walls and was suspended there when I looked in the closet. He shot right over my shoulder and knocked plaster down my neck. I pivoted very quickly and fired. Before I left the room, I picked his gun up off of the floor and I still have that gun to this very day. It's a German Luger.

There was a concentration of German soldiers up in the Hurtgen Forest and we were headed straight for them. We went deep into the woods, which is one of the most dangerous places to be during a battle because of the tree burst. When shrapnel hits the trees the wood burst into spears or large splinters and shoots out from the trunk. Tree burst can kill or mane. So we started digging a bunker, which is like a good size foxhole. I guess you could call this one a fox den. We dug the bunker into the side of a hill and put logs across the top to protect us from the possible shrapnel from the trees. Eventually, the Germans started firing eighty-eights over our heads. The wood and bark flying off the trees were hitting everywhere but the logs covering the bunker protected us.

Shortly after entering the forest we got called out and as we were rushing to get out, shrapnel from an eighty-eight sliced a leg off of one of my buddies. In this case there was no mortar fire to stop the bleeding. My buddy would bleed to death while waiting on a medic. He cried, "Oh God! Johnny help me." I had to do something, so I quickly poured some gasoline on the bleeding stub and struck a match to set it on fire. As my buddy was screaming and within a few seconds the bleeding stopped as the fire cooked the vessels. I put the fire out and left him there while hoping he would make it if the medics found him soon.

A lot of people lost their life in those woods. That's why it's now known as the "The Bloody Forest".

Chapter 10 - Headed for the Bulge

Even though we were in the middle of a big battle in the forest, trouble was brewing back in Belgium, so we were called out of the Hurtgen Forest battle and ordered to return to Belgium. In order to fool the Germans into thinking we were still there, we left a few tanks in the area. The tanks were instructed to idle their engines down the road then turn around and drive back. They were just to go back and forth to make the Germans think we were moving more tanks into the area rather than pulling out.

As we backtracked through Aachen the stench in the air was so heavy with the smell of rotting flesh, I could hardly stand it. We got through there as fast as we could. We were headed to an unknown destination in Belgium but ran out of gas as we got back to Liege.

Liege was a main railroad junction in Belgium. As we approached Liege, we were kind of relaxed while driving slowly along in our vehicles talking and telling jokes, but we were also on the lookout for the enemy. We knew we were running low on fuel and was looking for a place to set up a command post while we waited for supplies. Our convoy was slowly moving past a large railroad yard when a buzz bomb came over our vehicles.

There were two men elevated up on an anti-aircraft battery over the railroad yard about five hundred yards from a large locomotive. They were air attack gunners who started firing at the buzz bomb. Their job was to protect the rail yard from air attacks. The truck I was riding in was about a ton and a half (or a six by six) and was about three hundred yards away from the locomotive when the buzz bomb hit the engine. That buzz bomb came over the town of Liege and hit the engine, I mean just ka-boom! And it blew the curtains off the sides of my truck. It took us by surprise. The curtains on the truck measured about four feet by two feet and were pretty strong and it blew both curtains plum off and whacked me right across the face because I was sitting in the front passenger seat.

There were three of us in the front seat at the time and all three of us were scratched on the face. I received a scratch all the way across the face, and if I'd gone to a medic, I could have gotten a Purple Heart. I didn't want to waste the medic's time, so I didn't go. That's why most veterans don't think much about Purple Hearts because they were too easy to get. Some of the medals were given out when they shouldn't have been.

The two air attack gunners were both killed even though they were farther away from the blast than our truck. The concussion from the blast traveled up and out and killed the gunners, but just gave us a scratch even though those killed were nearly twice the distance away.

As we were moving through Liege, Spot, Chief's dog, was run over and killed by a GI truck. Chief had not yet returned to our outfit, and Spot had not taken up with anyone else even though he hung around with our trucks. It was like he was waiting for Chief to return.

There was a lot of German equipment just lying around all over the place in this one area where we were held up waiting for gas. Mayo thought he knew how a German bazooka worked. He was showing another guy how to use it while I was watching. This particular bazooka was about two inches in diameter and was about three and a half feet long. There was a dog nut on one end and about in the middle there was a button that was a little bigger than a thumb's nail and a key was holding it. Mayo was looking it up and down and turning it end over end and said, "You see, you point it this way, remove the key and mash the button to activate it and it will fire." He had the dog nut behind him.

I said, "Hey, that's wrong. The dog nut is what goes."

"Oh no, no."

I said, "I've seen a couple of them things and I know. It's the dog nut that goes."

"No, no. It goes just like I've got it. You're wrong."

"That ain't right, Mayo. Don't do that!" We were in a Chateau like area with a rock fence all around us.

"Yea, Yea. Well, I'm going to fire it."

"Well, I'm getting back away," and as I moved back he fired it. He mashed the button and was holding it and pointing it one way and when it fired, it went out the back end behind him and hit right at the base of the fence. It hit the gravel and burned his butt really good but luckily he wasn't hurt very bad. The rest of us had a good laugh. That's an example of the kind of crazy stuff GI's will do out in the field. There's not very much discipline. In the regular Army back in the states it's very disciplined. They even tell you when to go pee. But out in the field we pretty much did as we pleased.

I like to compare it to Teddy Roosevelt's Rough Riders. In 1899, Teddy Roosevelt is quoted as saying,

"For better it is to dare mighty things,

to win glorious triumphs,

even though checkered with failure,

than to take rank with those poor spirits

who neither enjoy much nor suffer much,

because they live in the gray twilight

that knows not victory nor defeat."

We were in a foreign country, and just like the Rough Riders, we didn't have a ranch (home) of our own but we had a job to do. So we just did the job one way or another or did whatever it took to get the job done. We tried things and they sometimes failed but we didn't give up. We just kept pushing and fighting. We were all from different backgrounds with different skills and had come together in the field of combat for a special purpose. We knew we were on our own because there was none of that close discipline. It's kind of like a buddy, buddy thing. We got' a do this and we got' a do that and we went and did it.

Also, in the field of combat you're never supposed to salute an officer. If the enemy is zeroed in on you and you salute, then the shot will go for the officer you saluted instead of you. So if you get pissed off at an officer all you've got to do is salute him, and that lets him know you're mad at him. If you really want to fire him up, just walk up to him and salute him. He'll say, "Oh no, don't do that!"

Ole Chief Kisto rejoined our outfit after recovering from his head injury. The Army couldn't afford to lose those "seasoned troops" with combat experience. He was upset to learn that Spot had been run over and didn't seem the same after that. He had really gotten attached to that old dog.

We were staying around a lot of Belgian people and they were trying to help us because we were running out of rations. We had been out in the Hurtgen Forest for so long we were really dirty and hadn't bathed in who knows how long.

Johnny washing clothes in gasoline, another GI watches.

The whole time I was in the war I don't think I washed my clothes one time in water. I washed them all in gasoline to kill the bugs.

There was this woman and her two daughters in this one town in Belgium. They wanted to feed us but our hands were really dirty. This gal told us she was going to wash our hands. So she got a brush and scrubbed my hands and then fed me with food she and her daughters had prepared. The food was greatly appreciated because we were staying hungry most of the time; the simple gesture of her cleaning my hands really touched me.

Around in this area a fellow from either A Company or C Company went AWOL for a couple of days, and their Captain Brown didn't want to court marshal him so he restricted him to the command post area. Captain Brown was a real good fellow but felt like he needed to punish the guy so he made him dig a six by six hole. This guy got really mad and went in and killed Captain Brown and his Lieutenant, and took off. Of course, the whole battalion started a manhunt looking for the guy. The orders were to get him. It just so happened that I was the guy that captured him. I ran right into him as I was going around a building. We ran head on, and I grabbed him and my trigger was half-gone. I almost shot him but I didn't. I hollered to the others that I had him and was bringing him in. As I was taking him back the other guys kept saying things to me like, "You damn fool. Why didn't you shoot him?"

I said, "No, we went out to capture him and we got him." I could have shot him and that'd been it, but I didn't because he wasn't putting up a fight. But if he had struggled to get away, I definitely would have shot him.

This was in December of 1944 and it was starting to get really cold. We eventually gassed up and left Liege and headed for Malmedy, Belgium. We were headed for the tip of the spearhead of the German Army. Hitler was quoted as saying he intended to have his Christmas dinner in Liege, and at that point he was twelve miles from it in Malmedy. It was colder than all get out. The 75th division had just gone in to that area around Malmedy and was getting ready for the next battle. The Germans had previously run over or defeated three of our divisions and taken many, many prisoners. Those divisions were the 28th Infantry Division, which was the first to go, then the 106th Infantry Division, and then the 7th Armored Division. We had word that the Germans had captured a lot of our troops, equipment, and supplies as we headed into the Battle of the Bulge.

Chapter 11 - Battle of the Bulge

The 75th division guys were ahead of us and had already settled into the Malmedy area. They were a division of green troops and hadn't seen much combat. It was getting late when we got to that point which was very close to the front. The 75th had a fire going, a big bonfire. It was so big we could see it far off in the distance as we approached. It was like they were having a weenie roast and we shouted, "Put that fire out!" Not in those words though, it was more like, "Put that damn fire out", is the way it went.

They shouted back, "Go to hell!"

So we said, "Okay, we'll go to hell." We turned our fifties towards them and fired over their heads. They did a quick job of putting out the fire.

After the fire was out, we went on up a little closer to the front line. We stopped our vehicles and it was very dark. There were no more fires or lights of any kind. Then they passed the word to bed down but to be ready to move out at anytime. I was glad at that time that Sergeant Harry Morrison made sure the squad truck stayed organized. So we got our sleeping bags out and bedded down.

We started listening to the radio and Propaganda Sally was on the airwaves. I found out after the war that she was an American named Mildred Gillars who was convicted of treason. During the war she had a reputation for trying to destroy the GI's morale by broadcasting propaganda messages nightly. Her official name was "Axis Sally", but we called her Propaganda Sally. We sometimes got a kick out of listening to her. She was really quite comical because she tried to sound like a sexy American May West. It was weird though when we listened to her because it seems like she knew exactly where we were. She would tell us which outfit we were in, where we were at and a lot of times call some of us by name, maybe even give our name and address. She would pick on the guys that were married by saying things like, "Have you thought about who your wife is sleeping with tonight?" She was trying to get our morale down. That was her job, to be a morale buster.

While we were bedded down there, Propaganda Sally knew that the 75th division had just moved into Liege and moved up front. She said, "We have already run over some seasoned divisions. Now with the 75th's green troops, do you really think you're going to be able to stop us?" She wasn't busting our morale. She was making us mad, and a mad soldier is hard to contain.

It seemed like we had only bedded down for just a very few minutes, then our squad leader Harry, hollered, "Let's go!" We moved on up on the line and started laying minefields and setting up traps to block the tanks. The Germans had recently made and just started using a new tank that we called "tiger tanks". They were made with six-inch thick armor and the seventy five-millimeter shells that we had would not penetrate that kind of tank armor. The shells would bounce off of the tank like hail bounces off the hood of a car and wouldn't phase its advancement. It would just keep on rolling.

It was real cold, and there was snow on the ground, which was frozen solid. Somebody said it was about thirty degrees below zero. We had to lay the mines right out on top of the ground because it was frozen too hard for us to bury them. My job was to put demolition on some trees that were along the side of the road.

As these big heavy "tiger tanks" were moving along the Germans were holding to the road mostly because they were afraid they'd get stuck out in the fields because they were so heavy. So they had to more or less stay on the roads. There was a wooded area with a little scope of pine trees that they had to go through. We were working in the dark and trying to be quiet while we worked. I was putting demolition on the trees to blow them in a way that they would fall into the road to block the tanks. While laying the demolition and mine fields, I was close enough to the Germans that I could hear them talking.

The only fire cover that we had was the 82nd Airborne and we understood that they were over to our right flank. We heard some small arms fire over to our right while we were working. That firefight lasted about five minutes, and then it quieted down. After that, there was no firing going on at all.

Our orders were to stop them one way or another. Junior Sneed and Mergenthaler were the bazooka people in our squad. They worked together as a team. One guy carries the bazooka and the other guy carries two satchel bags, which holds three bazooka shells in each one. Early that morning, and before daylight, they moved up closer to the tanks than anyone else in our outfit. They were sitting right along a fence line and next to the road; if the tanks moved out they would have a real close shot at them. The bazooka team would be our first effort to stop or at least slow down the tanks.

A little up the road from the bazooka was a seventy-five millimeter antitank gun and it would be used as our second line of defense to slow down the tanks' advancement.

There were a couple of guys helping me in the pine trees, and we got the job done and the demolition was set before daylight. Blowing the pines trees was our third line of defense to stop the tanks, and then we were to mount the tanks with Molotov cocktails. We had prepared Molotov cocktails and were planning to mount the tanks and set these cocktails off in their air intake that went into the engines. That would probably be the only way to shut the tank's engine down. Then they wouldn't be able to move, and that would have accomplished our mission. In addition to stopping them, we were also ordered to hold them up for as long as we could and hopefully until nine o'clock that morning. That would give our guys time to fly some more powerful antitank shells in from England that could destroy the tanks.

Our radioman was communicating with the commanders all the time and re-laying orders. Each company had a radio using dot, dot, dash and voice and stuff like that.

We had the trap set. Junior and Mergenthaler were lying in wait with the bazooka, the artillery was in place and we had demolition in the trees. Mines were laid around the road and we had Molotov cocktails in hand. Just before daylight, all we had to do was wait for the tiger tanks to come rolling up the road.

From my vantage point, I could see the antitank gun just up and around a short curve and setting across the road. We knew that our antitank shells could not penetrate that six-inch armor. I could see and hear the antitank gunner real good from the other side of the road. We heard the tiger tanks crank up and knew they had started to move.

Junior and Mergenthaler fired three or four bazooka shells right into the track of the lead tank, and that didn't stop it, it just kept moving slowly. It was moving real slow. It was moving so slowly that you could just walk along side and keep up with it easily. There were a lot more tanks behind this one that was leading the way. The other tanks were pretty far behind; I'd say at least a half a block behind.

The antitank gunner's officer told him to get ready to fire because the tanks had made it past the bazooka and were still on the move. And I looked over to this seventy-five millimeter antitank gun and the guy operating it had the thing aimed rather low. It looked like he was going to fire right into the ground. The officer said, "Get ready to fire and raise that gun, it's too low."

The gunner said, "No, I'm going to try something." He waited until the first tank got up pretty close to him. He fired and it ricocheted off the asphalt and hit the tank in the belly. It penetrated the tank and stopped it. It actually set the tank on fire. We were all really surprised because normally it would have just bounced off the side of its six-inch armor as it had done in other recent battles. So, that one shot hit the lead tank in the belly and stopped the entire convoy of tiger tanks. When the lead tank got stopped, it stopped all of them since the other tanks couldn't get by unless they drove out into the field. They must have been afraid because they didn't try to go around. They must have thought that their big heavy tanks would have probably gotten bogged down out in the field. Really, they probably could have made it because the ground was frozen hard. We held them up with that one shot and didn't have to blow the trees or mount the tanks with Molotov cocktails. That one man did that with that crazy shot he fired. And then we backed up a little and got a safe distance away and waited.

The shells from England showed up at about nine o'clock as planned, but they only had about three shells for each antitank gun. The shells were scarce due to a labor strike going on back in the states. Fortunately, the tanks were like sitting ducks. The antitank shells were moved up into striking distance and close enough where we could make contact. The first shell that was fired penetrated the six-inch armor like it was pasteboard.

That's as far as the Germans' drive got going towards Liege. They didn't move any further and Hitler's Christmas dinner plans were spoiled.

As we sat there and got organized and got lined up for a push we received more antitank shells. Just before we began to make the move we started getting some direct hits with eighty-eights or incoming artillery. The Germans were hitting some of our tanks, half- tracks and antitank guns. (Half-tracks are armored vehicles with tracks on the back and wheels on the front that steer.) It was direct hits. I mean just one shot and, boom! They hit their targets.

A fireplace in a Belgium house with a 49th Corps of Engineer's insignia, Christmas, 1944.

While we were getting this direct fire in, there were a bunch of small observer planes up in the sky. We could see about three or four planes and the commanders passed the word to everybody that these observer planes were L4 Grasshoppers. They're just little O' bitty small planes and were suppose to be friendly observer planes. They were right up over us and there were too many of them. The commanders knew that the Germans had captured a plane of this type, so they figured out that one of the observer planes had to have a German pilot. He must have been sitting up there looking at us, directing fire right in on top of us. But the other Grasshoppers up in the sky were friendlies and not knowing which one was the enemy caused a problem.

The commanders came up with a good idea. They gave the friendly planes orders to dive and get down all at once, and they gave us orders to fire on the one that didn't dive or come down in a hurry. Our guys in the Grasshoppers took a sudden nose-dive and were just skimming the ground. They came right down and the other plane was left up in the sky and not very high, about a thousand feet or less. So we fired on him, knocked his engine out, but he managed to land the plane. We captured the German sergeant that was flying the plane. After we got him down, we didn't have much more of a problem. Everything just sort of leveled off, but before that we were getting direct hits, just boom, boom, boom.

We were waiting one evening for the supply trucks to catch up and we noticed several German soldiers down and out in a field. We didn't know if they were dead or alive, but by morning and after a long below freezing night, one of their arms was sticking straight up in the air. We joked about it, "Hey, that guy's waving."

It was about that time when a lone soldier came walking up to our company and he told Captain Hahn that his entire company had surrendered to a German tank outfit when they were surrounded. The Germans made them all stand in a group and opened fire on them and left them all for dead. They all were dead except for this guy who was wounded and played dead until the tank crew moved out. When the coast was clear he started walking and found us. Captain Hahn gave the orders to go after the German tank crew and to take no prisoners.

We did exactly that. We tracked them down, destroyed their tanks and exterminated all prisoners.

We received the supplies we had been waiting for, except rations were still short, and we got plenty of ammunition and antitank shells. Then we began our move and headed towards Luxembourg.

We also got our mail. I got some letters and packages from Mary. My sweet Mary must have been trying to write to me every day. I also got some letters from my mom.

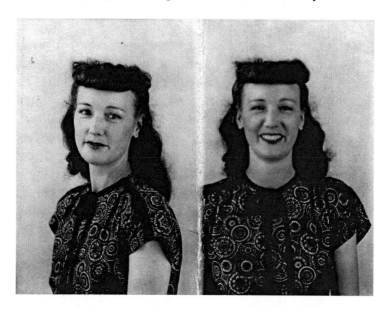

Mary sent me a lot of her beautiful pictures

Our tanks were sitting there behind us under cover and camouflaged. But when we started the push, our tanks had to get out into the open, so that made them more vulnerable. There were still a lot of German tanks and artillery in the area, so while the American tanks were moving the German tanks started shooting. A big tank battle started. The tanks were shooting at each other and their tanks were much stronger. Since we were in the open and moving, we lost about three to five tanks to the German's one tank. The Germans actually whipped us but we outnumbered them and kept on moving.

We captured a lot of German artillery and prisoners of war. Mixed in with the German prisoners was a guy who was obviously a civilian. He was a real rough looking mountain man about in his fifties who didn't have much clothing and appeared to be freezing and mistreated. It was very cold and the snow was knee deep. Because he was a civilian our MP's wouldn't take him as a POW. I felt sorry for the guy and brought him back to our CP, our command post. It was in a big barn like building and I fed the guy. He was very hungry, and he didn't have anywhere to go. He didn't speak French, he didn't speak German, and he didn't speak English. We had an interpreter there who figured out that he spoke Russian, but he could hardy speak his own language. The interpreter said he spoke some kind of broken Russian. I felt so sorry for him that I took him in to take care of him really. We ended up staying at that particular place for maybe a week.

Come to find out, this guy was a Russian who was working as a laborer with a German artillery group. He told the interpreter he was a mountaineer and the interpreter understood most of his lingo. The Russian said he was in his front yard chopping wood one day when a Russian army truck came down the road in front of his house. They forcibly strong armed him, picked him up, put him in the truck, and didn't even give him time to say goodbye to his family. They just loaded him up and wouldn't even let him get his coat he had laid over the fence while he was chopping wood. They made him help the Russian artillery crew. The Russians were using an older type of artillery, which required a large hole to be dug, and then they would back the big gun back down into the hole. This Russian man was helping dig holes, and the Germans had captured this Russian artillery bunch, which included this guy. I never did know his name. I called him Ruskie.

I asked Burbee, "Burbee, how about letting ole Ruskie here help you around the mess tent?" He agreed to let him help.

He said, "Yea, I could use him. He can help me load and unload trucks and do KP." So he worked down at the mess tent. We ate K rations and C rations most of the time. Well he did help by loading and unloading the truck, getting and setting up the cooking stoves, helped get the water and pulled trailers and all that. Burbee was glad to get him. The Russian took it upon himself not to eat until all the GI's were fed.

But when it came time for us to move, Captain Hahn said, "What are you going to do with that Russian?

I said, "Well, I'm going to take him with us."

"Why you can't do that, man. You're liable to start an international thing here."

I said, "Well, I don't care. I'm not even going to think about that, because I don't care about it. The man ain't got nowhere to go. What are you going to do but just leave him standing there out in the snow? He's going with us."

Captain Hahn said, "He's a civilian!"

"Well, I'm going to put him on a uniform." So I took him to the supply guy and I got him an American Army uniform that fit him and dressed him up like a soldier and put him on the truck. Ole Ruskie seemed happy about that. I guess he knew we would treat him good and he could work and earn his way.

After a lot of close up fighting with the Germans, I was feeling really nervous and jumpy. It seemed like Germans were coming at me from all directions. Even at night when I tried to sleep, I dreamed about being shot at by the enemy and woke up several times during the night in a cold sweat. I needed rest desperately, but we kept on moving, and we finally broke through and started to push up through Luxembourg. We went through the City of Luxembourg, which was one of the most modern cities I had seen over there. We didn't have much time to look it over, though, because we were on the move. The city was deserted. There was absolutely no one there. As we advanced towards Germany, we discovered that the Germans had put most all of the Luxembourg civilians out on the road to block our advancement. They actually sent them marching towards us to clutter up the roads to slow us down. Of course, my job was to clear the way.

Johnny and Sergeant Morrison   John C. Estes

Chapter 12 - Psycho Ward

It was right about this time when we got into Luxembourg that my buddies started noticing that I didn't seem right. They said I wasn't acting normal and was doing things like firing unnecessarily and was real jumpy or spooked easily. I felt like I'd get scared and fire too quickly and knew I was a little jumpy. So they sent me back to a Liege hospital. That was just about as bad as being on the front line. There were buzz bombs coming in all the time. So many people were being killed or wounded that there was a line of people waiting to be treated every day at the hospital.

They examined me in Liege and kept me there for two or three days and determined I needed to get further way from the activities of war. I was put on a plane and flown back to London. I believe I went to the Three Sixteen General Hospital, which was about sixty miles out of London. When I first went in they directed me into a barracks like place where the doors were locked. There were bars on the windows of the doors. It appeared to be a high security environment. There were ward boys in there that looked to be about six-six and weighted about three hundred pounds. They unlocked the door and let me in and seated me over in a waiting area. The doctor had gone to lunch.

I could tell I wasn't feeling right and knew that I needed rest, so I was okay about being sent to the hospital. There was a whole bunch of other guys already there that appeared to be having similar symptoms. The stove that was being used to heat the room burned coal and it had a screen around it so people couldn't get up against it and burn themselves. This place was obviously the psycho ward.

While I was waiting they brought in a guy that the ward boys had to hold because he was struggling to get away. They put him in a room right there close to the doctor's office. It was across from the waiting area where I was sitting. When they opened the door I saw that the room was padded. There was padding on the door, the walls, and everything inside was padded. And there was an examining table in the middle of the room that someone could lie down upon. The ward boys set this guy up on the examining table and held him while a nurse gave him a shot. They turned him loose, ran out of the room, and shut the door real fast. After the door was shut I could hear him holler every once in a while. In about five to ten minutes they checked on him and he was still in a rage and out of control. So the ward boys grabbed him again and the nurse came in and gave him another shot. They ended up giving him a third shot and that time when they opened the door he was passed out and lying on the floor. The ward boys picked him up, put him on the table, and wheeled him down the hall into another area.

There were a bunch of beds in the same room where I was sitting. One ole boy came up to me where I was sitting and looked at me. He got right in front of me and pointed his finger right down between my eyes. He bent over and got real close and he said, "They're going to get you boy."

He said, "They'll get you, they'll give you the needle, boy. They'll get you", all the while shaking his finger at me.

I said, "What do you mean they going to get me?"

This soldier, who was wearing a hospital gown, said, " You'll see, they'll get you."

I watched him turn and walk back into his ward. He passed another guy who was in a hospital gown and was sitting on the foot of a bed. That guy was holding a fishing pole that had a line on it. The line was hanging over in a bucket. He was fishing out of a two-gallon water bucket.

111

He was just sitting on the end of the bunk bed and fishing out of a bucket. The guy that pointed his finger at me bumped this guy's pole when he walked by. I mean that guy fishing just cussed him out and really unloaded on him.

It was at least an hour or longer before the doctor came back from lunch. After sitting in his office for a while he finally came in and spoke to me, "Hi, how are you doing?"

"I'm feeling okay, just tired."

"How long have you been here?"

"I've been waiting about an hour. I just got in from Liege, Belgium."

"How's everything going?"

I said, " I want to ask you a question first. Am I going to have to stay in this ward?"

He said, "No."

"That's a relief."

"I bet it is." Then he said, "I'm going to assign you to another area. You can go where you please. All I want you to do is just rest. You just have battle fatigue. If you get bored I've got a list of stuff that some people around here need help in doing. I know they would be glad to get your help. If you want to do it?"

I said, "Okay." So he gave me the list and I went on to my assigned bed. There weren't any screens around the stove. It was just a relaxing place. I could eat about anytime I wanted. I could go to the mess hall, walk around the mess hall, or do anything I wanted to except I couldn't go out of the gate unless I had a pass.

One time I went to the mess hall and there was a Sergeant who sat down beside me. He was a Buck Sergeant and he said, "I'm from the Third Armored Division. These damn people think I'm crazy but I ain't crazy. They're the ones that crazy. I'm going home."

After that he and I just talked normal about normal subjects and I got to know him pretty good. As we were leaving one day he lagged back just a little bit because

112

there was a guard coming with four German soldiers, POW's. While being guarded these POW's were working on the base in the hospital area. This Sergeant made it his business to walk between the guard and the POW's, which you're not supposed to do. The guard yelled, "Hey you damned fool! Don't you know better that to walk between me and my prisoners?"

Of course the Sergeant put on an act. He cussed the guard out and said, "I've killed better looking sons-of-bitches than you".

The guard went on and the Sergeant came up to me and said, "See what I mean. I act crazy as hell." He was faking it. I'm sure a bunch of soldiers like that were faking and acting like they had lost their minds in an attempt to go home.

From the list of jobs to do I picked a job to help a guy develop film. I just reported there when I wanted to for as long as I wanted to. I learned a little something about developing film, and he did seem to really appreciate my help.

We had to carry everything we owned with us everywhere we went. I had a barracks bag that I kept my personal belonging in that included my German Luger. One day, I asked for a pass to go into London because I was so bored. The pass was granted. I caught a bus and went into London. I strapped on the Luger out of habit. When I got off the bus there were two British MP's in the bus station, and of course, they saw that Luger hanging on my side.

The MP's said, "Hey, Yank. You got a gun in that holster?"

I said, "Yea."

"What is it?"

"It's a German Luger."

" Is it loaded?"

"Yea, it's loaded."

" Well Yank, you ain't allowed to carry a gun around like that here in London. So would you mind turning it in and picking it up when you leave?"

I said, " Who am I going to turn it in to? You?"

"No, you turn it into the American Provost Marshal."

"Oh. Well, I'll turn it in to him if he'll give me a receipt for it." They lead me down to the Marshal's office and I turned it in and got a receipt.

While in London I got lost. When I was ready to come home I didn't know where I was and couldn't find my way back to the bus station. I went to the Red Cross and asked for a room. I didn't understand why they asked me to pay. I thought the Red Cross was a charity organization that was supposed to help. It seemed to me that the room charge was either a quarter or a dollar and a quarter. I don't remember which. But it didn't matter because I didn't have the money to pay them no matter how much it cost. The Red Cross took my outfit number, serial number, and all my personal information and they deducted that room charge from my paycheck later on in the war.

The first night in London there was a lot of V2's coming in. I could tell they were V2's because the V1's made a whole lot of noise, like an airplane. But the V2 was a rocket that the Germans fired and it made no noise at all. A V2 is a ballistic missile and a V1 is a flying bomb. The V2 just hit and went ka-boom. There was no warning. You didn't even know it was anywhere around until it hit something. Two or three of the V2's hit that night. It blew the window lights out of the hotel where I was staying, the Red Cross's hotel.

The next morning I found my way back to the bus station, picked up my Luger, and reported back to the hospital.

After I was there for about thirty days, the doctor examined me again and wanted to classify me as either UK or ZI. UK was United Kingdom and ZI was Zone of

Interior, which was the United States. If they ZI'd you then they would send you back to the US. If they UK'd you then you stayed in the United Kingdom. So he marked me UK and I said, "What do you mean UK?" Of course, I was hoping for ZI.

The doctor said, "We're going to put you in the MP outfit in London."

"You mean you're going to have me patrolling Piccadilly Square?"

"Yea, that'll be part of your job."

"No! I absolutely refuse. I ain't going to do that. So far I've got a good record, but if you do that to me, you're going to run into one hell of a rough soldier. That's just the way it is. Either you send me back to my outfit or send me to ZI, one or the other. I'm not going to pull no MP duty on Piccadilly Square!"

The doctor said, "Well, your commanding officer, Captain Hahn, asked for you back when you came in here, but I've got to put you on limited service. You want me to send you back to your combat unit?"

Chapter 13 - Trip Back to Outfit

I sat there a minute seriously thinking about what the doctor said and then replied, "I don't care how you do it or what way you do it. That's the way it's going to be or I'm going to be one messed up soldier. You can depend on that."

He said, "Okay, I'm going to send you back to your outfit, but I don't know what in the hell they're going to do with you."

After signing a piece of paper stating that I volunteered to go back I was sent to a replacement depot and there was an officer, a Lieutenant, who was responsible for taking me and several other guys back to the front. All of us had already been in combat and it was really hard to get us to do anything. I was pretty much the only one that would pay attention to this officer. All the others just about did as they pleased. I felt sorry for the Lieutenant, and I tried to help him out on the way back.

My outfit had moved back up into Germany. This officer was assigned to take us all the way and these guys were giving him a lot of problems. I would say things to the other guys like, "There's no reason for you to be doing that." Or "Why don't you give the guy a break?" They kind of respected me I think because of that German Luger hanging on my side. They didn't have a gun that I knew of, and I did. So I joined sides with the Lieutenant because he was really having problems.

When we left the hospital, he took us to a boat. We left from South Hampton, England and landed at Le Harve, France. As we got off the boat we were marching to go on up to be bedded down for the night. One of the guys shouted at one of the sailors, "Hey, Swabie, you better go mop the deck."

The sailor answered back, "Damn dog face!" So this guy just busted out of line and headed for him and the Lieutenant had to grab him. That's just the kind of people he was dealing with and an example of the kind of trouble he was having with them. They had no discipline at all. How would you discipline a guy like that, anyway? It doesn't make no difference to him, you can't threaten to court martial him, because he doesn't care since you're making him go back to the front line. That's the reason there was no discipline because you can't hold anything over a person in that kind of situation.

We went on up and bedded down and that night some of them ran off and went into town where they got some booze. When they got back they were drunk and got in a fight with each other. I helped the Lieutenant break it up and finally he told them that he was appointing me as his assistant. That helped a little but not a whole lot. We still had problems.

We had made two or three moves to get back to our outfits. We went on up in the country kind of frog jumping up into where we were supposed to be. We stopped at a place because the Lieutenant wanted to give us range practice before we went back to the line. We went out on the firing range and they gave us .30-06 Springfield rifles. That's the oldest rifle that we had used in the war. The .30-06 was a bolt-action job and a real good gun. They wanted us to shoot in prone position. When we fired on the target we had to call our shot before the target goes down and is marked. That way they could tell if we knew what we were doing.

To call your shot you would have to say where you're going to hit. If you hit the bull, you called it bull's eye, six o'clock or twelve o'clock or dead center, or whatever. I laid down there in the prone position and set the sights. I believe it was a two hundred-yard range and I fired. I said, "Bull at six o'clock." Target went down and it was bull at six. I fired again and when I fired that time I said, "bull dead center". The thing went down and came back up and it was bull dead center. The range officer said, "That's all for you. You don't need no damn practice. You can get up now."

I said, "Man, I ain't done firing. Let me fire some more?"

He said, "No, that's it. Let somebody else get up there."

We eventually left the firing range and drove deeper into Europe and stopped for the night again. The next day the Lieutenant took us to another firing range. After what happened on the first firing range I thought to myself, "Why I ain't going to get to fire much anyway". While I was lying in prone position and waiting for instructions I could see right over the targets there was a big clay bank. Right over the clay bank you could see just about half of a house. I could tell it was damaged by artillery and it had a chimney that was sticking up over the hill. So I said to the guy lying along side of me, "Hey, I'm going to shoot at that chimney up there. I think I'll knock a brick off of that chimney."

He said, "I'm going to do that too. You fire first."

I said, "Okay". So I fired at that chimney and of course I knocked a brick off. Then my buddy fired and he also knocked a brick off. Well, when the other guys saw what we had done they all started firing at that chimney. I felt so bad about that because I was the one that had started it. I was supposed to be helping the Lieutenant and I was the one that caused the problem. In nothing flat, that old chimney just melted down to where you couldn't see it. The range manager kept shouting, "Cease fire, cease fire!" but they didn't pay any attention to him. They just kept firing until they fired all the shells they had in their guns. There were eight rounds in each one of them. The Lieutenant could only just stand there and shake his head.

We then moved on up and they scattered us out and I rejoined my outfit. The 49th had already crossed the Saar River in Germany by the time I got back. There were a few more guys missing and we had drawn some replacements or new guys but it was still pretty much the same. Ole Burbee said that Ruskie was really worried about me and asked about me all the time I was gone.

The Saar River was not a very big river but we had lost a lot of people crossing the river. The report to me was that the river actually did bleed and ran the color red because we lost so many. I didn't get back to participate in that. It was a small stream compared to the Rhine River where we were headed.

Chapter 14 - Feeding the Troops in Germany

The guys in my outfit were fighting with empty stomachs most of the time because rations were short. We were having difficulty getting everything Burbee needed to feed the troops. Being an outdoorsman and fisherman I was always paying attention to the streams we crossed. I got the idea to blast a stream to kill some fish. After all, I had all the stuff I needed. So I got a couple of German children that was hanging around to stand down in the creek where it was shallow to gather any dead or injured fish. There was a deep hole pretty close to where I was standing. A deep hole usually means there's fish close to the bottom.

My intention was to kill the fish with concussion. Concussion will spread over a large area as long as the blast doesn't occur near the bottom of the creek. The mud at the bottom will absorb about fifty percent of the concussion. I first tried throwing hand grenades in the hole and blasting the fish, but the grenades were too heavy and would sink to fast to kill the fish before they went off, and therefore, wasn't working too well.

I got another idea. I'd get a quarter pound box of TNT that I knew would float on top of the water. The box is about four inches by one and a half inches. I tied a string around the box and then tied a rock to the other end of the string and left about a three-foot length of string between the box and the rock. I lit the fuse, threw it in the water and the rock dropped to the bottom. Because the TNT box would float, it was three feet off the bottom when it went off and sent up a small blast of water. The concussion from the blast pretty much killed most of the fish in the hole, which came floating to the top. We ended up getting enough fish to feed the whole Company at one time. Most of the fish were carp or bottom feeders, but we didn't care. It was fresh fish.

When you're on the front line you mostly have K rations to eat. K rations came in a little box and had little bitty cans in it. It's easy to carry. The cans were smaller than a regular tuna fish can and had things in them like cheese, deviled ham or chicken. When we were in the "core area" which is back behind the front line we had C rations. They came in a little bit larger cans and you'd usually get two, one with some kind of meat and one with a side dish. It would be things like spaghetti and meatballs, corn beef hash or things like that. But back in the Army area they had regular canned foods, like carrots, beans and corn. They also had fresh potatoes, bread and meats.

Because of my efforts to bring in extra food during our tour of Europe, I had made real good friends with our Mess Sergeant Burbee. I was always trying to bring in wild game or domestic farm animals for him to cook, and of course, I had found him a pretty good assistant in Ruskie, who was still with us. Burbee started asking me to go back into the Army area and beg for food because the rations he was getting wasn't exactly what he wanted or needed, and there was never enough. He was especially interested in me being on the lookout for mustard seed. He wanted mustard seed to grind up and make hot mustard. Since I was supposed to be on limited duty it was easy to get Captain Hahn to agree to let me go see if I could get some food.

One day I noticed that my uniform had a second stripe on it. I have no idea when I was promoted to Corporal. It just showed up one day. It was like I earned it, and it grew on my arm.

I drove all the way back to the Army area and started hitting outfits, other companies and battalions, divisions in other areas, and it was mostly the Army people that were back in there. I'd ask them for any excess food that they weren't using. I took pretty much anything that they offered, loaded it up and drove back. I did such a good job that Burbee had me doing it all the time. I'd go to these depots where they'd issue the food out. Most of the time they had German troops, POW's, helping them. I acted like I owned the place. I'd walk right in and maybe give one of the Germans a pack of cigarettes. I knew a little enough German, and they knew a little English that I'd get them to understand that I wanted food. Sometimes I got my truck just loaded down on several occasions and not even have requisitions or any kind of paperwork.

Well we got the food anyway we could, and somebody would always go with me. At this one depot on the main road coming out of the area was a bomb crater. Trucks had to go real slow to get through the crater because it was kind of deep and it had water standing in it. I got this idea that my buddy and me would hide beside the road and when the trucks would slow down to go through that crater, we'd board the truck and throw stuff off. One time we got on one of the trucks that had a whole bunch of twenty to twenty-five gallon round pasteboard kegs. The kegs were real heavy, and we had no idea as to what was in them but we figured it was edible. So we started rolling a bunch of them off, then jumped off the truck and hide from view. When the coast was clear, we'd get our truck and load up the stuff we'd taken. The other GI's that were driving by would see us picking up boxes and barrels and kegs.

"Hey, what happened?" they'd say.

"We lost part of our load." Most of them would just go on by but there was this one guy who stopped to help and those kegs were real heavy. He worked very hard to help us load those kegs. We told him thank you and he left.

We did this a number of times and sometimes when we got back to our outfit we would find that they had moved. We'd had to run them down or find them because we didn't know where they had gone. When we got back to our outfit and opened these heavy kegs, it was cooking chocolate bars. They were just lying in the kegs and each one was about an inch thick and about three or four inches long. I don't know what Burbee ever done with those cooking chocolate bars. I don't remember ever eating any chocolate cake or brownies. We picked up a whole lot of extra food like that and even though rations were tight, we were eating pretty well.

One time when Burbee had made us a pretty good dinner, we went down in the basement of a house to eat and we were really enjoying the food. There was this new guy that carried a guitar that he had found in a German house. He could play any kind of instrument that he could get his hands on, but he talked a lot. He had a real big mouth. We were sitting there eating, and the new guy was sitting straddle a bench eating his dinner. This guy was yak, yak, yaking and yak, yak, yaking and yak, yak, yaking about much to do about nothing. I said to him, "Damn it! Shut up." He just kept on talking. I reached and got a twenty two-caliber target pistol that I had picked up along the way.

"Listen asshole, are you going to shut up?" as I held up the target pistol.

"No, I ain't going to shut up."

"You'd better shut up or I'm going to spill your coffee. I'll shoot a hole through your damn canteen cup." Us GI's really loved our coffee.

Johnny holding the German Luger

He said, "I don't believe you'll do it." And about that time I pulled the trigger and the doggone bullet just knocked the cup off the bench. The bullet didn't go through the cup. It dented the cup on the side, knocked it off the bench and spilled his coffee.

He stared at me for a minute then said, "I'm going to keep this canteen cup to remember you by." Everybody just laughed as we were setting there eating dinner. I shot at him and no one got excited about it. It was as if it was an everyday occurrence. Also, that twenty-two was just a popgun as far as he was concerned.

While in this area, B Company received orders to return to Huy, Belgium for special training. It took about a day to get there, and we stayed for about a week. The Navy had brought into Huy several, aluminum, landing size, crafts. These boats were pretty good in size and could carry several soldiers at one time. These landing crafts had twin cylinder, thirty horsepower motors. The Navy taught us how to operate the boats. We thought we were going to use them in an assault to cross the Rhine River. After the training we left the boats there and moved back up into the core area and just behind the front line.

All during this time we were in the core area and were assigned to different units. By this time the 49th was considered a bastard unit. We would only go into combat if they needed us. They would call us up, and we'd go in and do our job that needed to be done. Then we'd go back to the core area and the infantry would go in to the front line. So that's the way we worked. If they were stopped and ran into any obstacles that they couldn't move then we moved up and helped them get going again.

Sometimes they'd called us up to clear land mines. There is a crazy thing that I would always do when clearing minefields. First we had to find the mine with a mine detector. I'd sweep it over the ground until I located a mine. Then I had to get flat on my belly and probe around the edge of the mine using my bayonet, clearing dirt and being careful not to set the mine off. The detonator on a German mine was always in the center of the mine. Then I would dig it up. The crazy thing is that as I was flat on my belly with my face right up at the mine and probing with my right hand, I would use my left hand to cover my left eye. I thought that if the mine went off, maybe I'd save an eye. Fortunately, I didn't have to find out.

The Civilian Intelligence Core, CIC, was the boss in the Army Area and they controlled the towns and would put certain areas off limits to GI's, but in order to live up to our reputation we would find ways to get around the restrictions. If we wanted to go back to a town or a restricted area we would take a civilian automobile out of somebody's garage and paint the letters CIC on the side of the car and drive right on in to the town. Sometimes we would be challenged and our vehicles would be taken away, and we'd have to hitch hike back to our outfits. We were so mean that we'd get pissed off and swear to do something about it. One time there was a Sad Sachs cartoon in the "Stars and Stripes Newsletter" that pretty much summed it up. In the cartoon strip, ole Willie and his buddy, Joe, went up to the city limits of one town, and an MP was standing there and told them the town was off limits. Willie looked at his buddy and said, "To hell with it. Let's go capture a town of our own."

Chapter 15 – ALIVE and Banking on It

The Rhine River runs through the middle and splits the town of Koln (Cologne), Germany. When we moved in to Koln, we took half of the town up to the river. The American's were on one side of the river and the Germans were on the other side of the river.

Going into Koln the 49th combat engineers were among the first to arrive in the town. Our job was to go in and around the town checking buildings, looking for booby traps and making sure German soldiers was not hiding in the buildings. We cleared the place out and were waiting around for the main force to arrive. As we went down the streets we noticed a lot of store windows with mannequins dressed in clothes for sale and we saw a large military store that actually sold German uniforms. My squad got the idea to play another prank on the incoming troops. We went into the store and took a mannequin out of the window display. The mannequin had on a German officer's uniform. The dummy had a stand with it so we stood it right out in the middle of the street. We put the mannequin just around a corner. That way any incoming troops would only be able to see it as they turned the corner. Then we got inside a building and were watching out a window to see what would happen. The main force started arriving and as the pinpoint jeep turned the corner the gunman in the jeep swung his fifty-caliber machine gun around and looked real hard but didn't fire. That jeep just buzzed right on by. Then the troops in the next jeep that came around the corner pulled their guns and cut down on the mannequin and shot it up pretty good. We were laughing and got a good kick out of it. We were shouting things back like, "Are you a little trigger happy? What's the matter? You don't know a fucking mannequin from a real German soldier?" We were laughing and got a big kick out of it and so did the troops in the jeep that fired the shots.

They sarcastically shouted back, "Sorry we messed up your uniform," and then laughed and continued rolling down the street.

After having fun with the mannequin, the infantry went down by the river to set up an outpost on the front line. Our destination was Bonn, another large town down the river about twelve miles. That's where we thought we would eventually cross the river. Once again we had been moving so fast that we had out run our supplies. Being ahead of our supply line meant we had to hold up and wait. We waited there for maybe a week.

We were taking houses and other buildings for occupation. When we were going through France and Belgium we were mostly camping outside and avoiding civilians or trying to help them; and they were trying to help us. But when we got in to Germany it was a completely different story. We were running civilians out of their homes and using their cars and taking whatever we needed. We mostly operated under the rule to take and keep whatever we wanted that belonged to German soldiers or the German government but only borrow things from the German citizens unless, of course, it was watches, jewelry, guns or something you wanted to keep. Looting was part of the spoils of war and exactly what the German people deserved for causing us to be there in the first place.

Sergeant Morrison, playing around
with German hat in Koln.

I had heard rumors about a real big U.S. gun called Big
Bertha that didn't shoot artillery shells but shot a big bomb.
I had heard about it but had never seen it and neither had
anyone else in my outfit. We were staying in a German
house one night and it was dark and we heard some noise
outside. There was an open field right in back of this house
and everyone went outside to see what was happening. We
found out that they were moving in artillery. So we didn't
think much about it. Artillery was most often moved in
when it got dark and moved out before daylight. They had
moved Big Bertha in but we didn't know it. We heard them
out there talking for two or three hours and then we heard
this guy say, "Ready, fire."

When that thing went off, it blew all the window lights out of our house. We dove under the stove or table or bed or whatever we could get under. Then it quieted down and we went outside and found out it was Big Bertha. They fired it one time and started loading it again. That was the biggest shell I'd ever seen in my life. They had to load it with a crane.

While we watched they shot Big Bertha at the Germans across the river for the second time then threw camouflage netting over the big gun. It wasn't but just a minute that a German plane was over head looking for the big gun. We could always tell if it was a German plane by the noise of the engine and by the way it was acting. They were usually circling around as if they were looking for something.

Nobody fired on the German plane. I guess they had orders not to fire because it would kind of give away their position. The German plane was gone in about five minutes. Then they fired Big Bertha a third time. After that they started tearing the thing down. They only fired three rounds from that position and then they pulled out and left. That was the first and only time I ever saw Big Bertha because most of the time it was back in the core area.

Around about in Koln a good buddy of mine in the 49th, named Abshire, someone who had been with us from the beginning, turned up missing and was assumed AWOL.

Sometime in the past I had made friends with First Lieutenant Scoff, who was in A Company. He was from Nashville and somehow we ran into each other. I was always looking for guys from my home state. He was a fun loving practical joker kind of like me, except I think he was kind of crazy. He would do really crazy things. One day while in Koln, he dressed up in a German officer's uniform and started walking around out in a neighborhood. Before he did that the civilians were going on about their daily normal activities. They were walking up and down the streets or hanging laundry out on a clothesline or talking to
130

a neighbor. But when he walked by they dropped what they were doing and took off running indoors slamming the door behind them. I guess they figured somebody was going to come after the German officer and bullets would be flying. I guess they were trying to get out of the line of fire. It's a wonder he didn't get killed.

During the time there, our P47 fighter-bombers were making bombing runs over the Germans on the other side of the river. The bombers were flying three or four sorties a day and would always be in a squad of four. One time when I was up near the front line, there was a squad of fighter-bombers that went up and dropped bombs on the German front line. As they were on their way back, the German artillery fired and hit one of the planes. As the plane was coming in full force for a crash landing, two of the other planes flew up real close to the injured plane, one on the right side and one on the left side. They moved close enough that each had a wing under the injured plane's wings, holding it up and trying to help it glide into a field. It was obvious that the two support planes were struggling and desperately trying to help their buddy to the ground safely. There was a railroad track there and a highway ran right alongside the railroad track. The highway was a little bit higher elevation than the railroad track. Just on the other side of the highway was a large open field.

I looked up and could see these planes actually flying along side of this crippled plane. They were trying to lift him up to get him into the field, which was over on the other side of the railroad track and the highway. I could see that they were losing altitude very rapidly and for some reason the pilot in the crippled plane climbed out of his cockpit and moved out on to a wing. The planes got so low to the ground that the support planes had to turn him loose. The crippled plane hit the bank of the railroad and threw the pilot across the highway and into the other bank on the other side. We went running over to the pilot and tried

131

helping him. He was still alive. The other three planes circled and circled and circled. They were waiting around hoping to get some kind of message from us. So I got a big stick and wrote in the dirt behind the railroad track the letters A-L-I-V-E. After I wrote the message, ALIVE, the pilots waved their wings and went on their way. The ambulance got to us very quickly and they carried him away. For some reason I sat down and cried like a baby.

Shortly after the plane crash, Lieutenant Scoff came up to me and told me about a Federal Bank that was down on the bank of the Rhine River in no man's land. I was still feeling kind of down about the bomber pilot's crash, when he said, "Hey, John there's a bank down there that's probably loaded with money. It's a government owned bank and it's right down on the bank of the river."

"So what about it?"

"Well you got the demolition we would need. Let's go down there and scout it and see if we can make a run down there without getting into too much fire and blow that bank." I was just kind of shaking my head no and he continued, "There's a problem. It's pretty much out in the open. So the Germans would be able to see us pretty good."

I was still just sitting there and not saying much when he said, "Oh hell Johnny, Let's just go take a look."

So we drove down to the edge of the opening and scouted it out.

While we were sitting in the jeep, Lieutenant Scoff said, "I believe we can make it down there. We could just buzz right down, stay behind these buildings for as long as possible, which would take us as close as a city block from the bank. Then we'd have a direct shot to the bank, but we'd be out in the open."

I said, "Yea, they'd have a pretty clear shot at us. It's downhill all the way." I thought a minute then I said, "Oh hell, let's give it a try. Why not? I'll have to bring plenty of demolition because we might have to blow half the building down to get in there."

Real early the next morning we got ready. I grabbed some Composition C out of my demolition box and Lieutenant Scoff drove an A Company jeep over and picked me up. We headed out and drove the route we had planned. We drove real close to the buildings to stay out of sight up until about a block away from the Federal Bank. Then we made a run for the bank moving as fast as that jeep would go. We were hell bent on making it. The engine was running wide open and we made it to the bank without drawing any fire.

I took a deep breath as we pulled in behind the bank, which put us out of the line of fire, so far, so good. We jumped out of the jeep, ran around to the front entrance and were surprised to find the front door was open. It was standing wide open like the bank tellers had left in a hurry. I imagined that when the Americans moved in they cleared out as fast as possible. When we got inside it was set up pretty much like a regular bank. There was a real pretty glass dome up in the ceiling and a line of teller windows, which were surrounded by a heavy wire cage that was locked. We had to blow the cage door down, and I noticed that the blast did a little damage to the glass dome. When we got to the vault it was unlocked. All we had to do was to open it and walk in.

When I looked into the vault I could see money stacked up on the shelves. The vault was completely full.

"Good gosh, look at the money!"

Scoff said, "Only get the twenty Mark bills." The US military had declared that the only denomination that could be spent by the German population was the twenty-mark bill or lower. There was a freeze on higher amounts, so that's what we got. We each had a duffel bag and we started stuffing them full.

When the bags were full, we took off. We ran out of the bank and jumped in the jeep and started getting away as fast as we could. Evidently, we had surprised the Germans when we went down in there, but they were ready for us when we made our getaway. We were about two thirds of the way back up the block before we started receiving small arms fire. The bullets were hitting the dirt and the building in front of us but the only thing that got hit was a tire. The bullet punctured the tire but we were able to drive it all the way back to our unit.

The next day, Lieutenant Scoff came back, "Let's go back and get some more."

"No way, they'll be waiting for us this time."

"Oh, come on Johnny."

"No way, I ain't going to put my life on the line for that lousy German money that I can't even spend. I have absolutely no need for it."

"Well, I'm going back. I'll get somebody else to go with me if you don't."

"That's stupid man. You might as well get somebody else because I ain't going."

So he found somebody else to go with him and later on I asked him, "Did you make it back down there?"

"Yea, I did."

"How much money did you get?"

"We got a bunch of it." And that's all he said.

(I never did count the twenty mark bills I had but I estimate it to have been at least two hundred bundles of one hundred, twenty mark bills or approximately 400,000 Deutche Marks.)

Calvin's squad
Back row: Geary, Abshire, Varey, Hook, Fisher
Front row: Persinger, Estes, Morrison, Strait, Mergenthaler,
Guccaido, Sneed, Mohan
    In Koln, Germany early spring, 1945

Chapter 16 – Crossing the Rhine

We thought we were going to get the assignment of putting the bridge across the River Rhine, but we didn't. The 3rd armored engineer battalion got the assignment down in Bonn, which was twelve miles downriver. Our job was to get the boats ready to cross the Rhine at Koln. The Rhine was too deep, too wide and too swift to cross on foot. The nearest point across was over thirteen hundred feet. The Army had moved the boats from Huy, Belgium to Koln in big trucks in anticipation of the crossing. We started launching the boats and gassing them up and checking the engines and preparing to cross. While we were working, our artillery was shelling the opposite side of the river. They were really pounding them. Then we got the word that the boat crossing was going to be a decoy and that the actual crossing was going to be down river at Bonn. We were instructed to take ropes and tie the motors where they could only go in a straight line, then to start the engines and cut the boats loose.

We went down to the shore under a smoke screen that had been thrown down river by our artillery. I couldn't see anywhere through the thick smoke and felt like our artillery was covering us up real good. At the same time, the artillery continued to shell the other side. Of course, with all this activity the Germans thought we were going to cross right then and there. As a result, the Germans started moving troops and big guns and tanks in to the area just across the Rhine where they thought these boats would possibly land. They were just sure that's where we were going to cross.

Actually, our main forces were moving down river to cross at Bonn as the Germans were sending their forces up river and in the opposite direction to stop the boat crossing.

There were only about ten of the V boats but they were pretty big, about twenty-foot long. We called them V boats because the bow was shaped like a V.

Using ropes, we tied the steering to direct the boats as straight as possible across the river, cranked the motors and turned them all loose at the same time. I wish I could have seen the Germans faces when they found out that the boats were empty. We turned the boats loose at the time they specified and then we ran back as fast as we could, jumped in our vehicles and headed down river going towards Bonn, so we could also cross the river. It was early in the morning when we got to Bonn and found out that the original bridge had been intact when we captured it but had now collapsed. Our troops captured the bridge across the Rhine but the Germans had damaged it in some way. Before we got there a few vehicles had managed to cross before the bridge collapsed. That's why they were in the process of constructing a pontoon bridge when I arrived. My outfit crossed the Rhine in boats. Our job was to get over on the other side and protect the other engineers as they finished the construction of the pontoon bridge. We made our assault crossing with no problem at all. We didn't even get a small arms fire shot at us. One shell landed about in the middle of the river while we were crossing, and I don't know today whether it was enemy or friendly fire. I suspect it was friendly fire.

Pontoon bridge across the Rhine River

Using the pontoon bridge, the 1st Army managed to move across to the other side and formed a spearhead brigade that had been a long time plan of General Eisenhower's. We got our vehicles, tanks, armored cars, artillery, half-tracks, troops and supplies and everything else we needed across to start our long push or spearhead and shot up right through the middle of Germany.

Chapter 17 - Spearheading

My battalion broke off and became part of a small task force that moved out ahead of the main force. Our number one objective was to go into small towns and cut communications by knocking out the radio stations and cutting the power lines. We were zigzagging up through northwestern and northeastern Germany in the direction of Berlin using a topographic map. We didn't go in a straight-line. Our strategy was to keep the Germans guessing and to throw them off our trail. The Germans tried to confuse us by changing the road signs, but with the special maps we were moving pretty good.

We'd go into a lot of these little towns and tell them to turn all their weapons in immediately and every one of the civilians would pile the guns up. We'd load them on a half-track or truck and haul them out and then be on our way. A lot of times we'd go into houses in these small towns and would find wounded German soldiers recuperating or some that were on furlough. We'd just scare them to death as we walked in unannounced by busting the door down. We didn't bother them but ordered them to stay home and not to go anywhere. We issued them an official paper that stated they had surrendered.

We confused the Germans so much. They didn't know what in the heck was going on as we zigzagged up through the countryside. They thought the whole force, I guess, was behind us, but we knew our main forces were not close behind. It was a tense situation because we were expecting to run into major German forces at any moment. At one point we were at least one hundred miles out in front. We were so far out; the trucks that were to bring us supplies were getting ambushed. We had to slow down so they could catch up because when an Army or outfit runs out of supplies then they're useless as a fighting force.

As we were rolling along, the pinpoint jeep spotted a motorcycle coming as we had gone up a grade that curved back to the left. When the motorcycle was spotted it was on the other side of a little hill. The convoy stopped. The pinpoint jeep came back down the road and got out of sight. Our thirty-seven millimeter scout car moved up in front and lowered his gun aiming it right on the road. When the motorcycle appeared around the curve I could see a man riding in a sidecar attached to the motorcycle. The twosome continued down the road and when the motorcycle topped the hill, the driver probably saw us about the same time that the gunner fired. The shell hit the engine of the motorcycle that was right down between the driver's legs. The motorcycle and sidecar burst into flames and made a loud explosion but remained intact. Immediately after the blast the driver of the motorcycle was leaning over the handlebars and the sidecar passenger was leaning over the front of the sidecar. They were obviously dead. As the fire burned the bodies, they straightened up. They just sit up straight. I guess their muscles were tightening as they burned and the shrinking tissue pulled the bodies up into a sitting position. It was a strange looking thing to see.

Just a few minutes after that, I had another hair-raising experience. There wasn't any more traffic coming after the motorcycle was destroyed so we got back up on the road and started moving over the hill towards terrain that leveled off. We knew from looking at the map that there was a military school up on our left. We were concerned that maybe soldiers were in the school. Just before we got to a big arched gate going into the school grounds, a German military truck came buzzing down the road. It turned into the school. Just as it turned someone opened fire and hit the truck. The shooter was using small arms, maybe a fifty-caliber gun or a machine gun. The truck continued to make the turn after it was fired upon. We drove on up near the entrance, and I was one of the GI's that had to go in and

140

clear the place out. As we approached the arched gate, I could see a little courtyard with a driveway going up in front of the school. In the driveway the truck had stopped and the motor was dead. It was just sitting there right after the turn and obviously had run up against the curb and stopped. I moved slowly and cautiously as I approached the passenger side of the truck while keeping the truck between the building and me for protection in case someone was in the school. I opened the passenger side door staying back an arm's length or as far as I could. There to my surprise, was a blond headed woman, wearing a military uniform, lying down in the seat. She was facing me with her eyes wide open, staring back at me and was obviously dead. She had big blue icy cold eyes. I felt like they were piercing right through me. That raised the hair on my head and gave me cold chills.

We found nothing unusual as we searched the school building. There was nobody in the school building, and we found no booby traps. Once again we started on our way down the road and there was a movement up ahead and some trigger-happy guy fired his weapon. The entire convoy stopped. A horse stumbled out and fell in the middle of the road. We were held up there a few minutes to look the situation over to make sure there was nothing else, other than the horse. The horse had fallen on the road right in front of a house that set back in the bushes. A woman came running out of the house and up to the horse. She dropped on her knees behind the horse and took a butcher knife and cut out a whole bunch of round meat out of its back hips. Once she finished harvesting the meat, she wrapped it in her apron and went running back in to the house. When the house was checked we only found the female butcher and some old man. After that we drove around the horse carcass lying in the road and continued on our way.

One day we captured about a battalion of German soldiers. We spotted them off in the distance and threw a pincer around them. A pincer is what we called it when we surrounded the enemy and crushed them as we tightened the circle. The German commanding officer surrendered because he knew they were surrounded and didn't have a chance. Orders were radioed back to the main force to send MP's to take the prisoners. We waited quite awhile for the Army MP's to show up. It was maybe two to three hours that we waited. It took them that much time to get enough vehicles and men together to come and pick up the POW's. I don't remember whether they marched them back or hauled them back.

The captain of the German soldiers could speak real good English. I was standing there with Captain Hahn and the German captain and two or three other guys just standing around carrying on a conversation about the war and talking about the whole situation. As we were talking, a buzz bomb came over our heads. Of course, it was very loud when it was directly over our heads. A buzz bomb doesn't fly very high and it makes an awful bunch of noise. So we quit talking because we couldn't hear each other. I don't know whether it was headed for Liege or London or where but it was on its way and could travel over one hundred and fifty miles. After it quieted down and we could understand each other, I looked up at the thing and I said, "I hope that thing is headed for the top of the White House and blows the damn thing off so they'll know there's a war going on over here."

When I made that remark, this German officer clicked his heels together and came to attention. He looked at my captain and said, "You mean you allow your troops to talk like that?"

Captain Hahn stood there and looked at him a minute and he said, "Well, might be a damn good idea."

142

That German officer would not talk to us anymore. He shut up. If you asked him a question, he would give a short answer. He was not interested in talking. He didn't respect us anymore. The Germans were really disciplined and they were good soldiers.

I felt that way about the White House because I knew the people back there were living it up and enjoying themselves. I felt that they didn't realize that there was a war going on. The only problem going on back in the states was some rationing and I think there was one other thing in the back of my mind.

John L. Lewis, the President of the United Mine Workers of America, and his union members agreed to go on a labor strike. During the time of the strike our ammo was rationed. These union workers were supplying the coal that they needed to run the steam engines to ship the ammo and the big artillery shells. So what good is a soldier if he ain't got ammo? The strike had really jeopardized our efforts and possibility even extended the length of the war. What were they striking for anyway? Probably, they wanted increased wages or benefits for those coal workers not realizing the cost: the loss of more GI's. It was a bad time to go on strike; so most soldiers hated his guts. That really pissed us off at John L. Lewis.

Some days our progress was just unbelievable. Some days we'd drive as fast as thirty miles an hour. As far as opposition we just weren't hitting any at all. We were surprising the heck out of the Germans that we came upon or we were managing to avoid large German outfits by driving around their camps. Even though we were driving through thousands of German soldiers held up in camps we were unaware that they were there. We were cutting communications without much opposition. They didn't have any idea that we were within one hundred miles of them. After the war was over, Eisenhower said if he'd only known that we were running through that many German

143

troops that he wouldn't have dared to send us through there in such a small task force. It worked though, and it worked fine. It was the 1st Army, 3rd Armored Division that was the main forces. We were a part of that but had broken off into a small task force.

Chapter 18 - Liberators

As we got deeper into Germany and got into some small towns, we started running into camps. Some were POW camps and others were concentration camps that held mostly Pollocks. We freed every camp we ran across. We freed some British and American camps that had prisoners of war. The British and Americans were well fed and well dressed. They were clean and well taken care of as POWs when compared to the other non-POW camps and Russian POW camps.

The camps holding Russian POW's were not as well kept as the American and British camps. We came upon a bunch of Russian POWs, whose guards had disappeared. We left them there and went up near the Russian front line to inform the main Russian army about the camp. We lead a Russian commander along with several Russian trucks back to pick up the POWs. When we arrived back at the camp, all the Russians had left. A US interpreter that had waited at the camp said the Russian POWs didn't want to return to Russia, so they ran off. After that, when we ran into other Russian POWs we loaded them up ourselves and took them back to the Russian front line.

The other camps that held the Poles and the Jews were a whole different picture and told a completely different story. The Poles and Jews were treated lousy. We found dead bodies of men, women and children piled up or just lying all over the place. The stench was unbearable. The people that were still alive were barely alive and only skin and bones. Their clothing was a simple thin-striped suit, and they were living in filth. You could tell by looking at their faces that they had lost all hope and dignity. It was a struggle for most to even smile and laugh with joy as they received their freedom. I hated the Germans because we were there fighting them. Now I knew why we were there and I had a whole new reason to hate them even more. I know the holocaust really happened, but it's still hard for me to believe even though I saw it with my very own eyes. An Army communication guy took some pictures, developed them in a dark room tent he had set up and passed them out to some of the GI's. I sent a stack of pictures home to Mary.

When approaching the camps, we didn't meet any resistance to freeing the prisoners. The SS that was guarding the camps just melted away and disappeared and the prisoners kind of spilled out of the camps and walked into freedom. The Polish people that were coming out of the camps were so happy and proud to see us that as we drove by them it was like a celebration parade! They swarmed on the tanks and vehicles. They wanted to kiss us and shake our hands while celebrating with cheers and shouts of appreciation. It was like being attacked by a bunch of skeletons as we paraded past the camps. It was hard to believe my very own eyes and I felt so sorry for them but they were blocking our vehicles and it was my job to clear the way. As they were trying to kiss and shake our hands, we had to knock them off the tanks and trucks. We had to get them off to keep from running over them as we moved out towards the next unknown surprise. Whatever lay around the next curve in the road couldn't be any more shocking than what we had just witnessed. It seemed like we had paraded through hell and liberated the poor, condemned souls.

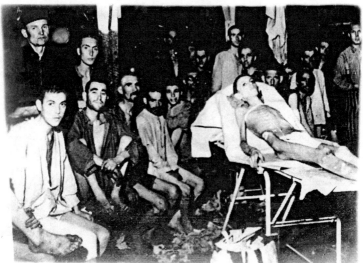

Slave labors in the Buchenwald Camp

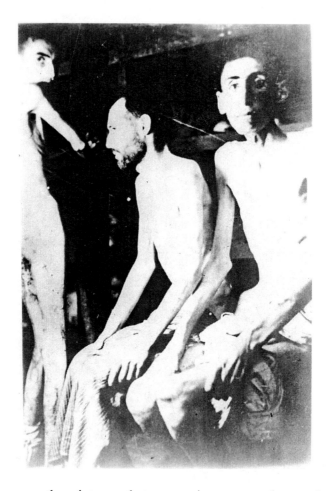

These are the pictures that were given to me by an Army communications guy. I'm not sure which pictures were taken at the camps I was at and I'm certain some of the pictures were taken at other locations. He just gave me a stack of pictures and these are the ones I sent home to Mary.

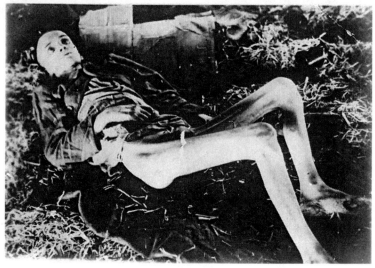

We were receiving orders either by radio or by messages being dropped from planes. We got the order to stop. We moved on up to another small German town which was the first town we stopped at and stayed for any length of time at all during this spearhead through Germany. When we arrived in the town, we asked for the Burgermeister. The Burgermeister is the mayor. A citizen pointed out his house. Because we were going to be staying around for a day or two, we needed to set up a command post, and the Burgermeister's house was just what we wanted. So we gave the Burgermeister maybe five minutes to move out. He came out of the house with a whole bunch of nice dress shirts and suits over his shoulder.

There were several freed Pollocks running around. There was this one particular Pollock, who said his name was Franciszek, standing there and he still had on a prison outfit, a thin, striped, dirty suit. I later found out that the name Franciszek is polish for Francis, which means free. So I don't know if that was his real name or whether he just said his name was Franciszek. I couldn't understand what he was saying but he was pointing at the Burgermeister and shouting something. So I stopped the Burgermeister and told him to give me one of his suits. He handed me one, reluctantly, and I offered it to this Pollock. Franciszek stripped off right there and put this nice suit on. He had this suit on and was strutting around there with it on like he was something else.

Then we moved into the Burgermeister's house. We just sat around and waited for our orders to move on and I guess we waited for about a week before everything caught up with us.

Hitler was in Berlin, and we were about fifty to sixty miles out at that point. We were sitting around there, and the Pollocks were just wearing the tar out of us. They had started raiding the German peoples' houses, going down into basements and getting food and clothing. We had to

158

quiet that down twice while we were there. There was no effort to organize these people that were released from the concentration camps. They were just scattered to the four winds. We didn't have time, and we didn't have anybody to take charge. We just set them free and that was it. So they were just around town and hungry. The guards working at the camps and running the place had scattered to the four winds also. I believe the freed Pollocks killed some of them.

We were sitting there one day and here come this Pollock still dressed in his prison uniform with a knapsack over his shoulder and headed towards the German line. I made the remark, "Hey that guy's going the wrong way," which looked odd. They were always going in the opposite direction.

The Pollock headed in the wrong direction saw us looking at him. Franciszek, who was always trying to help us out, heard me make that statement. One time, I even caught Franciszek trying to tie my bootlaces and stuff like that. They were trying to help the Americans all they could. Franciszek was with two or three other Pollocks sitting there and heard what I said. They turned around and looked when I made the remark that he was going the wrong way. The other GI's agreed something was wrong. Franciszek and the other Pollocks turned around and looked. They jumped up and ran out in the road and grabbed this guy and started beating the tar out of him. Some of us GI's ran out in the road where the fight was taking place and I pulled Franciszek off of what I thought was another Pollock. I got on the left side of the guy and another soldier got on the other side. We were just pushing and shoving these Poles off of him. I shouted, "Back up."

He didn't, so I turned around and hit Franciszek and knocked him down. He jumped right back up and grabbed me by my left arm. We were trying to protect the Pollock that we thought was going in the wrong direction from the other Pollocks that had jumped him. They jumped on him and were beating the tar out of him and we finally managed to pull them off. We lead this mystery Pollock towards the CP to get the interpreter to take care of the situation.

As we were walking towards the CP, Franciszek, who had several teeth missing in front, grabbed me by my left arm and swung around and hit that guy right in the mouth and knocked out some of his teeth. I knocked Franciszek down again. Come to find out this was an SS guy that had been guarding them over at the camp area. After we got the interpreter we found out what the deal was. Franciszek said that guy had knocked his teeth out, and he had sworn that he would get even with him. So he was very happy that he got to hit him in the mouth.

While we were in this area we would go on a few missions. We'd go up front and help them out a little, but we were mostly just lounging around. One day, one of our cooks hollered at me. He said, "Wait up! Wait up a minute! I want to show you something."

He showed me a German P38 pistol and he said, "I can buy this off of a guy for twenty bucks. Is it any good? Is it worth it?"

Well, I just took the thing in my hand and threw the safety on it and fired it right down into the ground. I fired it until I emptied it. Then I reloaded it and shoved the clip back in the thing and was holding it down towards the ground. The cotton-picking thing went off when I shoved the clip in the second time. The cook grabbed his knee and pulled it up and started hopping around and around and hollering.

I asked, "What'd it do, powder burn ya?"

A jeep driver that drove for the Captain was watching and said, "Hell, you shot him!"

I looked down then at his boot and his boot was full of blood. We grabbed him and threw him in the jeep and carried him up near the collecting point. About the time we

160

got to the collecting point, a firefight had started with some Germans, who were firing pretty good. We dumped him off right quick at the collecting point.

We jumped in the jeep to get the heck out of there because we didn't have a mission in there at all and wasn't supposed to be in there. When we dropped him off, the medic said, "Where'd he get it?"

I shouted, "Down the road!" That's all I said and we jumped in the jeep and took off.

I got a letter from the guy later before I left Europe. He said I'd done him a favor. He'd got discharged and awarded the Purple Heart. So that was what a GI calls a million dollar wound. It was about here that the main body caught up with us and we started packing up to move out.

As we were moving out we met the Russians at the Elbe River. The Russians were real hard to get along with. It seemed that they didn't have any discipline at all. Even though we were supposed to be allies we weren't mixing with them. They seemed to hate the American GI's, and we didn't like them much either. We were on one side of the river and they were on the other side. There was a Russian weapons carrier feeding down the other side of the river, and a guy was riding guard up and in front of the vehicle. He looked over at us and fired on us. I jumped up on the vehicle next to me and turned the old fifty on him, and I fired back. Boy, did I get called on the carpet for that.

Someone reported the incident to the CP and I got called in to talk to the Captain. Captain Hahn was chewing me out and said, "John, you could have started a damn international deal or something like that. What in the hell were you thinking?"

I thought to myself, "How many times have I been asked that question during this war? Then I said to him, "Listen, if you shoot at me, I'll shoot back. If my brother shoots at me, I'm going to shoot back. If a lousy son-of-a-bitch

Russian shoots at me, then I'm going to shoot back. And that's the way it is. I've got to do what I've got to do."

And he said, "You're a damn good soldier."

"Thank you, sir."

Captain Hahn then said, "Johnny, we've found Abshire." Abshire had finally been located after being AWOL for weeks. Before he came up missing he and I had become pretty good friends.

"We've got to send him back to the Army area for court martial. And John, you're going to take him back."

"What?"

"Yep, you've got the job taking him back."

I said, "Well okay, if that's the way it is. Sure there's no way I can get out of it?"

He said, "No, it's your job. Carry him back. Get him back there for the court martial." So I got ready to go and put him in the front passenger seat of the jeep. I rode in the back because I had a jeep driver. Also, by riding in the back I could keep a better eye on Abshire who was handcuffed. We took off. It was about a couple of hour's drive to the Army area where the court martial was to take place. While we were riding along, Abshire turned to me and said, "Johnny, when we get up here in this little town and slow down, I'm going to jump out and run."

I said, "No you don't Abshire."

"Yes, I'm going to do it. You can just let me go and say that I escaped."

"Abshire, you know that if I let you get away then I'll have to serve your time. You understand that don't you?"

He said, "Yea, I understand that but you can fire at me and all that and maybe you wouldn't have to serve my time."

"That's a big maybe, Abshire. So understand this, if you run then the first shot will be at your knees, and if you keep going after that, then the second shot will be right between your shoulders. Don't forget that and don't try it."

162

He acted surprised and then said, "I really believe you'd do it and after all we've been through together."

"You know I'll do it because I ain't fixing to serve no time for you or anybody else. I'm going home as soon as I'm released."

So I carried him on in for the court martial and he was sentenced for a very long time. During the court martial, I had to sit outside and wait. When the court martial was over, Captain Hahn and another officer came out of the room. Captain Hahn looked at me and said, "Fix bayonet."

I asked, "Why?"

"I said to fix beet. You're taking charge of this prisoner. He has been sentenced." So I fixed bayonet and they brought him out and turned him over to me and I had to carry him over to the designated area. That's the last time I heard from ole Abshire. I don't know what happened to him but I delivered him and I sure didn't have to serve his time.

My mother was a worrywart and when I wrote to her I was all the time trying to reassure her that I would be all right. So I wrote her the following letter and mailed it, which was postmarked on April 8, 1945. She was so proud of it that she had it published in the Nashville Newspaper.

A SOLDIER SOMEWHERE IN GER-
MANY

Dear Mom and Dad:

Ill drop you a few lines to say hello, and to let you know I am just fine. I hope this will find you and dad well and O. K. Mom, I just returned from church. I am glad to say that I really like to go to church, and I do every chance I get. Whether it means a long walk or a long cold ride in a truck, I go when I get the chance, and I in tend to keep it up from here on out. I have read my pocket testament through and going over it again, and I find every time you read it you al- ways get something new out of it that you didn't quite understand the first time. Mom, I know it makes you feel better to know I am going to church, reading my testament and praying and mom, with you, dad, Uncle Willy, grandmother and Mary praying for my return home—well, I would like to ask you one question, how can I lose?

Mom, I know you worry a lot and you know that wont do any good. If the Lord sees fit for me to return, well, there's only one answer. I'll be there some day. Mom, I feel that every- thing happens for the best. Just re- member there's a better place to meet your friends and loved ones than in this old world. So mom, leave it to God and quit worrying. What do you say? O. K.

Well mom, I'll say so long for now, and I'll write again tomorrow. So keep your chin up and answer soon.

T-5 JOHN CALVIN ESTES.

I wasn't just making up the stuff about church to reassure my mother. I felt that it was my belief in God that had protected me this far and I wanted to hold on to that comfort for as long as I could. Therefore, I attended "Stump Services" whenever they were held. Each company had a Catholic and Protestant priest that accompanied us during the entire war. They would hold services even if we were on the front line. Almost every soldier carried a new testament in his pocket. We'd find a stump or log or big rock to sit on while we listened to the service. That's why we always called them Stump Services.

On April 12, 1945, President Roosevelt died. We found out about it the same way we found out about anything happening in the world, through the Stars and Stripes. It was sad that he didn't live to see the end of the war, but other than that it didn't affect the GI's at all. We still had a job to do. A German POW asked me, "What's going to happen now that your leader is dead?"

I said, "It's not going to make any difference. Someone else will step up to take his place. Think about it as if there is a very large post sticking up out of the water in the middle of a pond. If you remove the post, the water will fill in the space and you won't even be able to tell there was once a post ever there."

Chapter 19 - Nordhausen, Crows and Bicycles

When we arrived in Nordhausen, I was astonished to see so many bicycles. I have never seen as many bicycles in my life as there were in Nordhausen. There were bicycles at every house and all over the place.

We had advanced close enough that we ran into the first German air defense ring around Berlin. Hitler had set up several air defense rings to defend Berlin and to make his last stand. So when we crossed over the first ring near Nordhausen we ran into some major trouble. The Germans stopped us cold.

Our convoy was moving along a road and our pinpoint jeeps were frog jumping. The enemy fired an aircraft shell at our convoy and knocked out one of our pinpoint jeeps. Instead of the Germans having the air attack guns pointing up in to the sky, they had lowered them to ground level. So we turned around in a hurry as they continued to fire aircraft shells at us, but they missed even though they were firing point blank or real close.

We got back as quickly as we could and stayed back for a couple of days to regroup. We had stopped right by a little ole creek. It was a real nice place with small cabins right along the creek. We stayed in the cabins and sent out patrols to see what we were running into. There was a barn about a thousand yards off from where we were, with a field in between the cabins and the barn. We were sitting around and enjoying the scenery and relaxing and decided to clean our weapons up a little bit. It was so relaxing that I was doing a lot of yawning and stretching.

On this beautiful quite spring day, I was taking my time cleaning the barrel of my weapon, which was a "Browning Automatic" also known as a BAR. I was sitting there and looking through the sights and looked out in the field. Through the sights I could see a crow had landed on an old plow handle way out in the middle of this field and about half way to the barn. It was unusual to see a bird of any kind during this war. It so happened that the plow was in line with the barn, and there was kind of a bank there where I was setting. So I casually stood up and that made the bank about shoulder level. I laid the barrel of the Browning down on the bank, and cut down on that crow to see if I could hit him. Bullets were ricocheting off the field and off of the dirt and the bullets were hitting the barn. I didn't hit the crow, but I shot some of the handle off of the plow, and therefore, fired at the plow handle several more times.

In just a few minutes one of the guys said, "Good gosh, looky here!" There came a whole platoon of German soldiers walking towards us with their soft hats on and with their hands over their heads. They had been hiding out in the barn and thought I was shooting at them. It was very funny to me and reminded me of old Alvin C. York during World War I. He had single handily captured a bunch of German soldiers. I was thinking and laughing to my self that must the way ole Alvin C. York captured all those people.

A little while after that we had set up a water depot. Some of my buddies and me were getting some water. We were on the side of a road pumping water out of a pond through a filter and into jugs. One of the guys said, "What is that a coming here?" So I got up on the truck and stood up on the fifty-caliber gun and said, "Good gosh, them's Germans!" I jumped down from the truck and about that time a whole platoon of German soldiers were riding bicycles and heading directly towards us. They didn't even know we were around as they rode right on down where we were along the side of the road. We dropped the water jugs and pointed our weapons towards them, as they got closer. We captured them with no resistance. There were forty to

167

forty-five of them and only four of us. Strange things were happening all the time.

In this area I was clearing houses and found a woman dressed in a German military uniform. I took her to see Captain Hahn. He was standing in front of a house talking to another commander. I said, "Captain Hahn, what do you want me to do with this woman?"

He said, "I don't care. That's your problem."

"Well, Captain, I don't have any idea."

Captain Hahn said, "Just take care of her." So I thought a minute and looked at him and he just stared back at me. I then marched the woman around to the back of the house. I stepped back and raised my gun. She was crying. I then shot two rounds into the ground and told her to get gone quick, "Vex schnell!" She took off. I went back to the front of the house and Captain Hahn's month was hanging open and he said, "I didn't tell you to shoot her."

"Well, you told me to take care of her, didn't you?" and I walked off. I never told him any different. If he didn't go around to the back of the house, he probably thinks to this very day that I shot her.

We started moving out of the Nordhausen area and going though little old towns. We were doing our job, going from door to door and building to building in the middle of this one town, right down on the main street. A German plane came on the straightaway and started bombing. For some reason Chief Kisto got right out in the middle of the street. None of us could understand why he did that. The rest of us dived inside of the doorways to get out of the way of the bullets and bombs. It looked like that bomb hit ole Chief right on top of the head. It went right at him and went ka-boom. When the dust had cleared away we could see Chief lying in the street. We ran out to him, picked him up and put him in a meat wagon. Miraculously, he was still alive, but he was messed up pretty badly. They carried him back to a hospital. We heard a month later that he was still alive but I don't know if he ever made it home.

Chapter 20 – Roll Out the Barrel

After doing all this spearheading and pushing through Germany, we moved back to a little old town by the name of Friedeburg, Germany. It was a real pretty little town with a big chateau right in the middle of town that had a nice courtyard. There was an old church mission in town, which I visited several times. I wanted to make sure God knew how thankful I was to have made it this far. I was scared I'd get knocked off by some stupid bullet just when maybe the war is about to come to an end.

We became the military government for that area which included the surrounding areas. We were the only authority that was recognized. Our orders were to just keep order, maintain peace, pick up stragglers and turn them in to the stockade in Eisleben. Eisleben was a town just a few miles up the road. One of the main industries in the area was a large brewery located in Eisleben. The brewery had been shut down because of the war and a large majority of the population was out of work due to the brewery closing.

We used the chateau that was right up on a hill as our headquarters or command post. There was one person who owned most all the land around the chateau. The chateau employees that lived in houses around in the town were still able to work at the chateau. Every morning they would meet in a barnyard for their assignments. A big blond-headed woman, who was around fifty years old, owned the chateau and she could speak good English. Her husband was an officer in the German Army. While we were there we never heard from him as to whether he was still alive or what happened to him. She was trying to boss us around quite a bit and I resented that. She and I didn't geehaw too much. I got into a little argument with her one day about the way she treated an old man that worked for her.

Gravel
Girty

Sketch by Viola

This old man watched the cattle and fed the horses and took care of other livestock. He rode around on an old mule. He was also some kind of a night watchman and he was a real good old fellow. I guess he was probably in his mid to late sixties and he was a real good friend to the American troops. He helped us out quite a bit. The owner of the chateau was giving all the workers a hard time and I said, "Hey, don't be so damn hard on the workers."

She said, "It's none of your damn business."

I said, "Shut your damn mouth! You old Gravel Gertie looking thing."

She looked at me real funny and said, "Don't call me Gravel Gertie!"

I said, "Just go in the house and shut up!"

"Well," she said, "I'm going to tell your Captain!"

I said, "Good, that'll be fine. His office is right over there." So I followed her over to Captain Hahn's office.

She called him out and said, "This soldier here said I looked like Gravel Gertie." He looked at her a minute and then he looked at me. Then he scratched his head and looked back at her and said, "Damn if he ain't right. You do remind me of Gravel Gertie." Gravel Gertie is a Dick Tracy comic strip character that was introduced in September of 1944. This character had big bug-eyes and a very pointed chin and long blond hair. I didn't have any more problems with that gal.

She had a guy that worked for her that the workers called the Gestapo, who also spoke English. He was over all these farm workers like a foreman. He rode a horse and wore tall boots and riding britches and dressed real good. He would assign jobs to the people that worked in the field. They worked long days while he rode around on his horse and policed the area. It appeared to me that he was real mean to the workers and didn't treat them very fairly. I watched the way he treated them for two or three days and didn't like what I saw.

172

And at this particular spot we were picking up stragglers coming out of the woods, the woodwork and everywhere. We were working real hard carrying prisoners to Eisleben because there was a large prison compound there that covered several acres. However, the compound was filling up fast because there were already a lot of prisoners captured. One time I'd picked up three German soldier stragglers, two men and one woman. She was the equivalent to a US WAC (US Women's Army Corp) and was very attractive. I carried them down to Eisleben to turn them over to the guy in charge of the stockade. He said, "I can take the men but I ain't going to take the woman. I ain't got room for her."

I asked, "What in the heck am I going to do with her?"

"I don't know what you're going to do with her. It's your problem." So I took her back to Friedeburg, which was only a few miles away. I took her over to Headquarters and found an interpreter. She said she had an uncle that lived there in that area. By that time it was getting kind of late, so I got permission from the executive officer to let her go to her uncle's house. When I was about to turn her loose our First Sergeant, Jack Terrell walked in to the CP. He hated the Germans regardless as to whether it was a child, woman or man. He'd just as soon shoot them as to look at them.

Jack had run into some screaming melees down on Normandy beach and was kind of beat up a little bit. The German's fired three of them at one time and they're mostly morale busters. They just scream and make a real loud noise, and of course, when they hit they go boom. One melee hit him and knocked him across the road, and then the next one hit him and knocked him back to the other side of the road. When he got up his nose was bleeding and he was pretty banged up. It kind of knocked him lou-lou. Jack seemed offbeat for the rest of the war. As some would say, "He lacked about four bricks having a full load." He was with Headquarters and I didn't see him much; but at this time I could see that Jack was a walking arsenal and was carrying a lot of ammo. He'd carry maybe six hand grenades on him at all time, and a bandoleer with about five clips that held eight rounds each, and he liked the grease gun. That was an automatic weapon that fired forty-fives. He carried it at all time. He wouldn't carry his carbine; he carried that grease gun.

Anyway, he saw this German girl there after I'd just got through talking to the interpreter. The interpreter said that the uncle lived just about a block from there and that he was a shoe cobbler. She knew where he lived and how to get there and it was getting late. So I told her to go on up there to her uncle's. Jack saw her leaving, and he grabbed that grease gun and flipped the lid back and was ready to fire. He had a look of hatred in his eyes when he walked passed me and towards the door. I knew he was going to shot her as soon as she went out the door because she was a German. The only weapon I had on me at that particular time was the German Luger. So I drew the German Luger right quick like and stuck it in his back and I told him, "Jack, if you fire, I'll drop you right here."

He stopped in his tracks dead cold and said, "You wouldn't do that."

"Pull the trigger and I'll show you." The girl saw what was happening and I shouted, "Vex schnell! Vex schnell!" That's German for get going fast. She really took off and got away. She headed towards her uncle's house. The executive officer was standing right behind me, pretty close, when I put the gun in ole Jack's ribs. He never opened his mouth. He never said a word. So Jack flipped his top back on his grease gun and I re-holstered my gun and we went on our way. That was all that was ever said. The next morning the executive officer who was second in command walked by as I was sitting out in the courtyard eating breakfast. He walked up to me and put his hand on my head and said, "You really meant that last night didn't you?"

I said, "You better believe I did."

He said, "Rough night, real rough night" and walked on off. And that was all that was ever mentioned about that incident.

I finished my breakfast and decided to find the shoe cobbler and check on the girl. She was very pretty and very frightened, and I wanted to make sure ole Jack hadn't tracked her down. I found her uncle's house; stepped up on the front porch, knocked on the door and stepped back down on the ground. The girl came to the door and stepped out on the porch. She spoke some English and understood that I was concerned and was asking how she was doing. Looking up at her I said something like, "You doing okay? Do you need anything?"

"Yes, okay. I'm fine. Thank you for protecting me last night."

"You're welcome. Ole Jack's a little crazy." I turned and started to walk off the porch and she said, "Wait, I have something for you." She steps back in side and came back with a loaf of bread and a bottle of liquor.

"Why think you, but that's not necessary."

"Please take it. It's the least I could do. My uncle is very old and he is thankful that the Americans are here." She steps off the porch to hand me the bread and liquor. There was a big open field near by, and I kind of looked out in its direction because I didn't know what to do or say. She looked that way and then said, "Come." She took my hand and we headed for the field. We walked pretty far out into the open field of barley. The fields were beautiful and went on for hundreds of acres. The mild breeze seemed to be inviting us to go deeper into the field and the soft green barley opened its arms and we sat down. I laid my rifle down on the ground beside me and moved around a little to find that perfect spot. We opened the bottle and shared the bread. We sit pretty close together talking about the war, the weather, and just enjoying the peace and quiet. I thought about Mary and was missing her real bad, but getting closer to this lovely German girl was very tempting. I thought about it being such a long time since I had touched delicate soft skin as I reach for her hand. She smiled and my soul was drawn into her face. Just as I was leaning in to kiss her, I heard a noise coming from behind me. I turned and looked as three armed German soldiers walked right up on us within about fifteen feet. I looked up at them and they just stopped and looked at me, then looked at the girl. I said, "Morgen."

They said, "Gut Morgen", then looked at each other and then back at me. This time they didn't take their eyes off of me.

I hesitated a minute then said, "Vex schnell!" and they took off quick. I don't know why I said what I said or did what I did. I was out numbered, so I believe it was pretty good thinking on my part. If I had of gone for my gun, the three of them could have taken me easily. I was out in the field about a good city block from the rest of the guys. Maybe they knew the war was about over and were headed home. With that happening, we picked up our stuff and headed back to town.

The girl headed towards her uncles, and I went back over to the chateau. The Gestapo was back at it again mistreating the old man as well as the other farm workers. The workers were lined up in the yard and waiting to get their assignments for the day. There was a young boy about fifteen or sixteen years old standing in the line. The boy said something to the Gestapo in German. The Gestapo walked over to the boy and shoved him real hard in the chest. Then the young boy said something else and he shoved him again. I saw all of this happening. I just walked over and grabbed that Gestapo by the collar and shoved him back up against his horse. I told him, "Today you're going to operate this guy's hoe."

The young boy was holding a regular garden hoe in his hand, and I said, "He's going to ride your horse and be the Gestapo."

He said, "No, No" and protested.

"Yes he is too. That's the way it's going to be today."

He said, "I don't have to do that."

"I know that. You don't have to do it, but if you want to be here tomorrow, you better do it today." So I gave him the hoe and put the boy up on the horse. I got an interpreter out there to tell this German boy to make sure he worked all day. I said, "When he stops, you holler and make him go. I'll be patrolling the area in the jeep." I said to the Gestapo, "If I see you stop working I'm going to drop your ass right there." That boy setting on the horse really smiled. He really liked that and the other workers did too. They headed out to the field and he walked right along with the other workers, and the boy rode the horse. That night when the Gestapo came in I checked his hands, and he had several blisters. He really did work all day. I felt good about making that dude work.

Our commanders had met with the Russians. They had agreed to a time when they would take over the occupation of this area in Germany. In the meantime, we had to occupy our time.

My squad was just hanging around one day. We were wishing we had some beer. One of the guys said, "I wish the brewery down in Eisleben would start making beer."

Another said, "Let's go down there and find out why they're not in operation."

"Hey, that's a great idea, let's go down and talk to them." We got an interpreter to go down with some of the guys to find out who owned it. They went to the Burgermeister, and he set up a meeting with the

Brewmaster. After the meeting the guys came back and said, "All they need is money and they'll get started."

Someone else spoke up and said, "Well, we ain't got that kind of money."

I said, "How much do they need? If it ain't too much, let's get it going." No one had any money, no one except me. I still had all those German marks that were taken from the bank. I had just been carrying the duffel bag around and stuffed behind the seat of the truck I was driving. The guys in my squad knew that I had the money from the bank. I really didn't need it for anything and had no plans around spending the money. I thought it certainly wouldn't be good for anything back in the States. So I agreed to pay all the bills and the employees at the brewery with the money. I handed Harry Morrison, the Platoon Sergeant, some money and he took it to the brewmaster. That's all it took and we got it back in operation. That brewery was putting out some good beer. They were bringing it in to the courtyard at the chateau in five gallon barrels. They would put the kegs right out on the ground in the center of the courtyard. Then as we needed it, we ordered a dump truck load of crushed ice and dumped it out on top of the barrels right out in the courtyard. We had good cold beer any time we wanted it.

The old night watchman that worked for Gravel Gertie helped out by taking money and delivering it to the brewery. I gave him money about three or four times to take to the brewery. I'd roll some Marks up in an old paper sack and he'd take it to the brewmaster. All the towns people were happy because they were back working and getting paid either by working at the brewery or for a supplier to the brewery. The GI's were happy because they had all the good cold beer they could drink. That brewery put out some pretty good beer.

At this particular place we had found a trailer that was used for a bus. All the buses over in Europe were mostly trailers that they used to haul people. The trailers looked
178

just like regular buses, only they were trailers. We got this thing and brought it in and set it up in this courtyard. We striped all the seats out and made a little bar room out of it with tables and chairs. The game room is what we called it because we'd play poker in there most of the time. It was so nice inside that guys would be standing in line to get into the trailer to play cards. We were able to fix it up very nicely because if we found something we wanted to use, we took it.

The brewery had been up and running for a while when we got the word that the war was over. It was early May 1945 and Hitler was dead and the Germans had surrendered. I had once said that on the day that they announced that the war was officially over I was going to dig me a foxhole and get in it. I really wish I had because all the guys were shooting off all their weapons and running and shouting everywhere. They were shooting out windows and it sounded like the 4th of July. It was a celebration. Everyone was acting like they were going to get to go home the next day. The war was officially over and dog gone it we had plenty of beer for the celebration. Actually, we knew we were assigned as military government so we were going to be around for a while and until the Russians took over.

After the excitement was over we had to get back to the same old stuff and we stayed there for maybe two more months.

Chapter 21 – Conquerors

We were getting ready to pull out of Friedeburg because the Russians were finally about to arrive. The game room was our pride and joy and we didn't like the idea of leaving it behind for those damned old Russians. When we were getting ready to leave, we decided to take the game room with us. It would be easy to move because it was originally a transportation trailer. It was on wheels and could be pulled behind a truck. So we tied the game room behind the truck and I got the job of pulling the cotton-picking thing. For some reason, the guys put me back on the tail end of the convoy and we pulled out of town and headed towards Eisleben to set up another command post. After all, that's where the brewery was located so we could have our beer delivered to our new command post and create a similar set up as we had in Friedeburg.

We hadn't gone very far at all when who did we meet but General Hodges. He saw that rolling bar on the back of my truck and at the tail end of the convoy. It kind of stuck out like a sore thumb. General Hodges' jeep made a quick turn around and came back and pulled me over. He said, "Soldier, drop that thing off right there! That's an order. Just unhook it and leave it there."

Without argument or hesitation I said, "Yes sir!" and I jumped out of the truck. I ran around to the back, unhooked the game room and left it right there on the side of the road. As I pulled out to catch up with the convoy, the Game Room abandoned on the side of the road was a sad sight to see in my rear view mirror. I'm sure the Russians got some good use out of it because it was left right there on the side of the road like a welcome sign coming into town.

We moved into Eisleben to set up our headquarters. We had our barracks or where we slept set up in some kind of school building. Everybody was milling around and there wasn't nothing much going on. The war was definitely over. Since I had made friends with a lot of the locals because of the brewery business, they were always trying to help me out. The local barber was after me to come by and get a hair cut, so I decided to take him up on his offer and walked across the street to get the haircut at his German barbershop.

Normally, we cut each other's hair. Fisher had some clippers that we would use but most of the time our beard would grow longer than our hair. During the war we would go for days without being able to shave or trim our hair. So I thought it would be nice to get a good shave and haircut.

Because the electricity was out the barber was right out on the street cutting hair. I pulled a chair out on the sidewalk and the barber started cutting my hair. About when he got through cutting my hair, a soldier told me that my platoon Sergeant, Sergeant Shuffler, Lieutenant Love and Captain Hahn wanted to talk to me at the command post. I immediately headed over to the office, but as I approached the road I had to wait for a motor pool to pass before crossing to the other side. It was General Hodges and his staff, again. I don't know if he recognized me from the rolling bar incident or not. He ordered his driver to stop and said, "Soldier, Where in the hell is your weapon?" He was chewing my butt out, again.

I said, "I just walked across the street to get a haircut and nothing's going on. The war's over."

He said, "I know the war's over, soldier. We won the damn war and are here now as conquerors and I don't want to see you again without a weapon! Act like the conqueror that you are."

"Yes, sir!" So I made sure I was wearing my weapon from then on and at all times. General Hodges drove off and I continued on over to the command post.

When I walked in to the office there sat my three commanding officers, "Yes, sir, Captain. What would you like?"

The Captain said, "You know damn well you're not suppose to fraternize with these people."

"I ain't fraternizing with nobody."

He said, "The guy's out there cutting your hair."

I said, "How in the hell can I fraternize with him when I don't know German?" He said, "Well, I've got to warn you of it and don't do it no more."

I said, "Okay." It was hard not being friendly and social, especially when all the locals wanted to shake my hand.

We were in Eisleben for at least a month when we got the orders it was time to leave. The Russians were moving in to this area as well. I drove my truck back down to Friedeburg and around town looking for the old night watchman to say goodbye and to give him a gift for being so kind and helpful. I found him riding his mule down the street and I called him over to the truck. He dismounted the mule and walked up to the truck. I reached in the duffel bag behind the seat in the truck and handed him two bundles of twenty Mark bills. I said, "I just wanted to say thanks."

As he flipped through one of the bundles his hands started shaking. He said, "That's the most money I've ever seen in my whole life".

I said something like, "Well." As I watched he broke out in a sweat and wiped his face with the front of his sleeve. He had the look of shock and surprise on his face. I just stood there watching him for a moment.

I thought what the heck and said, "Man, you want some money? I've got a bunch here that I don't know what I'm going to do with." So I reached back behind the seat and brought out the duffel bag and pulled all the money out a few bundles at a time and stacked them up on his arms like cardboard. That old man stood there with his arms out and loaded down and cried like a baby. The old man was

182

speechless and didn't say a word. He just stood there with his mouth open and cried. I don't know what he ever done with the money or whether he got to use it or not, but I hope he did. As I pulled out, I wished the old man good luck.

Chapter 22 - Too Many Points to Go Home

We moved into Ruin, France and the Army started assigning us to our next job. Some of the guys were being shipped to the Pacific, but I had too many points to go fight the Japanese. I had enough points for discharge and if I'd been in the ZI zone or the United States, well I'd been discharged immediately, but I was over there and the ships were being used to transport troops to the Pacific Theater. At that time, they had no way to send the GI home, who had enough points for discharge.

I got put in the "closing out forces" is what they called it. They were taking my outfit and busting it up in to six men teams. In other words, we had such a rough reputation, character and everything else that they busted us up into small manageable groups and shipped us out into different organizations.

While we were waiting around, I ran into Lieutenant Scoff, "Hey, John, you going to volunteer to stay on for awhile longer?"

"Hell, no, why would I do that?" I wanted to get back to my wife and a normal life.

"Well, they were asking for volunteers to stay on for another six months. So I took them up on that offer."

"Man, you're crazy. I'm going home."

He asked, "What are you going to do with all your money?"

"What money? I ain't got no money." So I told him the story of what I'd done with the money and he said, "You damned fool. I'm volunteering for another six months so I can stay and sell my money half price to incoming GI's headed into Germany."

I said, "Well golly, I never thought of that. I guess I'm just a dumb nut. But I don't care I want to go home." No doubt he made a lot of money.

I did have some business to take care of before I could ship out. I had to do something with Ruskie. He was still with us and needed to get home. I checked with the Red Cross and at first they didn't want to help because of who he was. When I told them I'd pay for his train ticket they agreed to guide him home. My problem was the ticket cost one hundred dollars. A ridiculous amount of money in those days and, of course, I didn't have that kind of money and neither did ole Ruskie. So I started asking everybody that had gotten to know ole Ruskie to help out and a lot of the other guys and me made up the money between us and bought him the ticket. Burbee packed Ruskie a little sack of food to carry on his trip. I reckon the Red Cross took care of him. I don't know if he ever made it home.

I got shipped to Brussels, Belgium for a few days and then ended up in Antwerp and stayed there for the rest of my stay in Europe. The six of us in this group from my outfit that was sent to Antwerp wasn't assigned any duty for quite awhile. Most of the soldiers stationed in Antwerp had not been in Europe for very long. They were "green" hadn't seen much action and were there for the closing out period. The new guys respected us combat veterans and pretty much did as we said. It was like being on vacation and we were free to come and go. We were sleeping in a six-man tent and I was the only experienced soldier in my tent. One night we were trying to go to sleep and one of the fellows in the tent had a light on and had been reading the same letters over and over again.

It was getting late when I said, "Turn that light out. Will ya?"

"I will when I'm finished reading my letters again."

"Man, you've got one minute to turn that light off or I'll shot it out."

"You wouldn't do that?" About that time I pulled my Luger out and shot the light."

He said, "Damn, I didn't think you'd do it!" He was startled.

A minute later a guard came up and stuck his head in the tent and said, "I heard a shot from over here. Where did it come from?"

One of the guys said, "What are you talking about? I didn't hear anything." The guard looked around the tent suspiciously, and then left.

While in Antwerp, the Stars and Stripes let us know about the big bombs that were dropped on two cities in Japan. I really didn't understand the magnitude of what it was all about. I just thought the government had developed a really, really large bomb using similar technology as in the past. And that bomb could level an entire city and kill hundreds of thousands of people at once. I thought it was a good thing and don't remember any GI thinking that it was not. We all thought it was better to drop the thing to stop the war rather than continue as it was and lose hundreds of thousands of our boys. Therefore, we were happy with the results.

During this time, I meet an old boy by the name of Sergeant Jones over at the motor pool. He and I got to be pretty good friends. When our Commanding Officer was transferred to another unit, they needed someone to take him to his new assignment and then go by and pick up our new CO who was in Lyon, France. Officers overseas were not allowed to drive vehicles, so they had to have a driver wherever they went. Sergeant Jones asked me to do it. I said, "No thanks, I don't want to go pick the guy up. I don't want no part of it."

The Sergeant said, "Well, you're the only guy we've got that I think will know the way down there and back. I need you to go." Finally he talked me in to going.

Early that morning, I got in my jeep, picked up the old CO and drove to Lyon, France. It was an all day drive and we arrived after dark. I dropped off the old CO and found a place to spend the night. The next morning I picked up the new CO and it was another day's drive back to Antwerp.

Early during the drive I was yak, yaking with him and he made a remark, "You don't have to make conversation with me."

So I said, "Okay." I didn't speak to him again for about three hundred miles. If he asked me something, I would answer him just as short as I could and that was it. The drive was so boring I was driving just as fast as I could. The CO said to me, "MPs are going to pull you over."

I said, "I don't care." That's all I said. I just wanted to get back as soon as I could.

We got into Antwerp and the way we were suppose to get to where we were going was through a tunnel. He asked, "Do you know where the tunnel is?"

I said, "Yea, I know." I was real short with him again. I brought him on to the outfit and the next day he wanted to call all the troops in and talk to each one personally. There were about two hundred people in the Company. He asked me, "What are you assigned to do?"

"I'm not assigned to nothing really. I go down to the motor pool ever once in a while and help Jones out."

He said, "Well, I want you as my personal driver."

"Hell no! No way."

"Why not?'

"Because I don't like to be around brass. You asked me now I've told you."

"Well, John you're my personal driver." His name was Captain Coursey. So from that day on I was his personal driver and I got the command car and drove him wherever he wanted to go. During this time, I also became the dispatcher for the motor pool. Captain Coursey turned out to be a real good officer. I took him in to Brussels one time

187

to an officers' get together that was being held at a big officers' club. The brass wanted to go and of course they had to have a GI drive them, so I had a carload of officers. It was so crowded in the car, they were pretty much sitting in each other's laps.

One of the officers asked, "Johnny, what are you going to do while we're in the Officers' Club?"

I said, "I'll sit out in the car and wait, I guess." I couldn't go in because I wasn't an officer.

So Captain Coursey said, "I'll fix that for you John, don't worry about it." So when we got to the place where the officers' club was at, Captain Coursey reached in his pocket and pulled a cap out that had Captain's bars on it. He put it on my head and said, "Captain Estes, come on let's go in." I had the hat on that had Captain's bars but my jacket didn't have any stripes on the sleeve. We went in and had our drinks and fun and what's so have you and went on back. They could have gotten me for impersonating an officer. Like I said, he turned out to be a pretty good Joe.

While we were at Antwerp, a Chaplain came by and asked permission to spend the night with us and to eat chow, and of course, the Captain said fine. We were standing there talking and Captain Coursey asked the Chaplain, "Where are you headed?

The Chaplain said, "I'm going down to Holland. I'm hitchhiking."

I said, "I've always wanted to go down in that area and look around."

Captain Coursey said, "Well you're the dispatcher. Why don't you dispatch you a vehicle and carry him down there?"

I said, "You know I hadn't thought about that. I believe I will. Chaplain, what time would you like to leave in the morning?"

"Right after chow."

"Okay, we'll go." So we took off the next morning down the coast. We followed the coast all the way down. It was a beautiful site. The flowers were in bloom. I couldn't see any grass. The whole area was covered with beautiful flowers. The landscape would be completely yellow on one side and red on the other. It was really beautiful. I drove him in to Holland and that's where his mother lived. He stayed there a couple of days and I went to the nearest Army outfit and got me a bed and stayed with them until he got ready to leave. He told me what day to pick him up and then we went back to Antwerp. I really enjoyed that trip.

Chapter 23 - Red Ball Convoy

I drove Captain Coursey around for a couple of months. Everything was constantly changing. Guys were being reassigned and our forces were shrinking. After a while I was assigned to another outfit and was working in the office of an S4 Officer, a Captain. He kept nagging me to lead the Red Ball Convoy because I had the most experience with the roads in Europe. The Red Ball Convoy was a spin off from the Red Ball Express that operated during the war. But I did not want to lead the Convoy or have anything to do with it because I associated the job with the black guys we had the run in with back in France at that bar. I just had a bad taste in my mouth with the GI's running the Red Ball Express during the war.

The Convoy was set up to haul war supplies to the ports and put them on ships to send to the Pacific. Then they would bring back other supplies and things that were needed to support the troops during the closing out period, such as food, cigarettes, clothes and blankets. Whereas, the Red Ball Express was the GI's lifeline and I always said, "What good's a GI, if he ain't got no supplies." The Express delivered fuel, ammo, supplies, equipment and the mail to troops during the war and was discontinued in November 1944.

After a lot of persistence on the Captain's part, I finally made a couple of runs with the Red Ball Convoy. Afterwards, I said to the Captain, "I'll lead the convoy if you let me pick my drivers."

He said, "That's good. You can select the drivers anyway you like."

I said, "I'll take a driver on a run and if I don't like him, when we get back, I'll fire him and find another one."

He said, " That's good," so I accepted the job and by the second or third trip I made I'd be gone some times five, six, seven or eight days from the outfit. Then I'd come by the outfit and get orders to go somewhere else.

The number of trucks varied depending on what we were hauling. Sometimes there would only be five or six trucks and then other times there could be as many as sixty to seventy trucks in the convoy.

The black market was big business and we had to constantly be on the look out for people trying to buy or steal our cargo.

One time I went into Liege, Belgium with a convoy of about fifteen to twenty trucks. We were hauling gasoline in five gallon cans and the trucks were stacked full. We came upon a steep grade going up hill and the trucks were pulling pretty hard. When we reached level ground, I saw a beer joint or pub and radioed to the boys, "It's time for a break." We pulled in and every driver went in to get a good cold beer. Some walked up to the bar and others found a table. I sat at a table. There was a local in the bar when we arrived who was real friendly. He offered to buy us a drink. Of course we took him up on the offer.

This guy came over to the table where I was setting and pulled up a chair.

He said, "Where you headed with that load of petrol?" He spoke good English.

"Liege. What's it to ya?"

"I'll pay you 800 Belgium franks for each five gallon can."

I stared at him a moment while my mind was quickly calculating eight hundred times approximately three hundred cans. I calmly asked, "You got that kind of money?"

He pulled out of his pocket a wad of money like you wouldn't believe.

I asked, "How are we going to unload it?"

"I'll take the trucks up the road and unload them and have them back within a couple of hours with empty cans on them."

I said, "Let me think about it."

I got up from the table and walked over to the bar and stood between a couple of my drivers.

"See that guy sitting over there. He's got a wad of money and wants to buy our gas and sell in on the black market. What'd ya say? Let's figure out a way to get him out back and take his money then make our delivery as scheduled."

While we stood there trying to put together our plan to mauver him out back, he got wise and took off.

We decided to get out of there before the guy came back with some friends.

By the time we got into Liege it was time to eat so we stopped at a transient mess hall. We had to park a pretty good distance and take a public trailer ride over to the mess hall. We got into the rear trailer and some civilian women riding in the front trailer saw us and started knocking on the window and waving. We didn't have any idea who they were. The guys and I were talking to each other and figured that no one around us could understand English. I said, "Who in the hell is that damn bitch? What in the fuck does she want?" Except I was using much nastier words. Me and the guys were kind of laughing and I said, "Where in the hell is that transit mess? We should be getting close."

A woman standing next to me wearing a uniform said, "It's on the next corner, you need to get off at the next stop."

When I looked down at her I could see a maple leaf on her left shoulder. That indicated that she was Canadian. I took my hat off and said, "Lady, I apologize for talking like that and I apologize for my group here."

"That's all right. I've been over here long enough, I've gotten used to it."

192

"Thank you and once again I apologize." I was embarrassed.

So we got off at the next stop and the women that had been waving at us got off too. It turned out to be the woman and her two daughters that scrubbed my hands and fed me during the war. I spoke to them a few minutes then we went on into the mess hall.

The Captain called me to his office one day and said, "I want you to go to Le Havre, France and pick up a load of supplies."

I said, "Okay" and he handed me two requisitions.

I said, "What do I need with two?"

He said, "You get your load from the first requisition, come back and sell it where ever you can and you split the money with me".

I said, "Now wait a minute," and I pulled up the chair closer to him. I looked him right in the eye ball and said, "Now you mean you're giving me the second requisition, so I can get it, sell it and distribute it any where I want?"

He said, "Amiens, France is a pretty good size town so your mark is good right in that area. That'd be about where you'd have to spend the night anyway. You can unload it and come on out of there."

I said, "Okay." So I took the two requisitions and I headed for Le Havre, France. Got my load and headed back towards Amiens and just before I got into that town, I met a jeep, an MP. And he flagged me to pull over and then he went up and turned around and pulled up in front of me and parked. He said, "Is your name John Estes?"

I said, "Yep"

He said, "I've got some orders for you."

I thought to myself, "That lousy son of a bitch, he done turned me in."

I said, "What's the orders?"

The MP said, "I've got to take you to the Provost Marshal 's office and you'll get your orders there."

"Okay."

"Just leave your vehicles here and I'll carry you in and we'll get the orders from there." So I went into the Provost Marshal's office.

The PMO said, "You've got a change of orders of where to deliver this convoy."

"What is it?"

He said, "Paris, France. Here's the Captain's name and address where you should report as soon as you get there." We took that convoy on into Paris and when we got there we found out that this Captain was the warden over the US Prison in Paris. We were able to drive the trucks into the building and up to a loading dock. As we were unloading, I could see that the prisoners were lined up to have supper. They were standing about three feet apart and it appeared that they weren't allowed to get closer than that to each other. The prison guards were holding billy sticks and staggered on each side of the prisoners. These prisoners were U.S. Army soldiers that had either deserted or shot somebody intentionally or committed some other kind of crime during the war.

They were Federal Prisoners and one of them kept looking at me. As I was working, I would look at him and he'd be looking at me. His face looked familiar but I didn't recognize him. He said something to the guy up in front of him and the guard standing near him warped him right across the back with that billy. It sounded like a big stick hitting a log. The guard said, "Shut up. You ain't supposed to talk in line". Later I thought that maybe it was ole Abshire.

That scene at the prison gave me a chill and made me realize how bad I wanted to get home and how necessary it was not to get into trouble. Well, we finished unloading our vehicles and I had more orders to go to another place. We drove to the next place and picked up another load and carried the stuff to a different location. I still had this spare

194

requisition for the goods that we first loaded. I made two or three runs all across Europe before I got back to my home base.

When I got back to home base it was pretty late. Being very tired I went straight to bed. The next morning I went down to the S4 section and told the Sergeant I wanted to see the Captain.

He said, "Okay."

He hollered at the Captain and said, "John's here. You ready to see him?"

He said, "Yea, send him on in." I went on in there and shut the door and drug my chair up pretty close to him and handed him that spare requisition.

I said, "Captain, you can get you another convoy leader if you want to, I got feathers on my legs and I ain't going through with that."

So he just took the requisition and he said, "Okay, that's fine."

I said, "Could I recommend somebody to take my place?"

He said, "No. You've still got the job." I don't know until today whether he really meant that or whether he was just trying me out, but he knew that when we were on the road that we would be carrying those extra supplies and everything. There were all kinds of temptations to make an extra buck.

We were supposed to be eating at GI places where we would have to sign tickets for everything we ate. But we didn't eat GI food most of the time. We'd go in a restaurant and give them a blanket or carton of cigarettes or something off the trucks and pretty much got to eat anything we wanted. He would have known we were doing that because he wasn't getting a whole lot of them food tickets back in, and naturally, he knew we were swapping stuff for food. I believe he was just trying me out. I just really believe that's what he was doing.

Chapter 24 - Skin It Back and Milk It Down

One day a letter was passed around to everybody that simply said that if you have eighty-five points or more then report to the office. I had more than that many points, so I reported to the office and they sent me to a staging area in Le Havre, France. We were assigned to a certain barrack and each one was full of guys headed home. The atmosphere was lively and everybody was happy even though we had to be quarantined there for a few days before we could ship out. There I was processed for shots and received a physical examination.

Several of us went in at the same time for the exam and to get our shots. First thing we had to do was to strip off all clothing and go through the medical line to be examined. It was the same way as when they inducted us in the Army at the Smyrna, Tennessee induction center and the same thing we had to do about every two months during the war. The doctor was sitting in a chair at the end of a line of naked GI's. Each guy had to walk up to him and when they did; he'd say the same thing, "Skin it back and milk it down." When the doctor said this to a GI in from of me, he replied, "Doc, if you'll smile at it, it'll skin its self back."

Of course, we were having our usual laughs and making crude jokes when it was my turn to step up in front of the doctor. When I walked up to him and started to skin it back he looked real hard at my penis and screamed, "God damn, scabies!" and everybody in the whole building heard him.

I said, "What the hell do you mean? Scabies?" I had one little red bump that probably looked like a chigger on the end of my penis and that's what he was calling scabies.

I said, "What's a scabie?"

He explained, "Well, it's kind of like lice or something like a chigger. You're a country boy so you know what a wolf is that gets on a rabbit. It gets under the hide."

I said, "Yea".

He said, "It's about the same thing."

Dec. 19-45
Nash. Tenn.

Dear Mary:

Will drop you a few lines as I am thinking of you. You sweet little headache, I have been dreaming for the passed few days that I was back in your arms to stay and I hope I never wake up hon. Will close for now. All my love, hugs and kisses, Johnnie

Then he said, "Your whole company up there in your barracks is quarantined now for two more weeks and we're going have to spray the place." They sprayed the whole barrack and we had to draw new clothing and he gave me medication to use. The medication cleared it up in nothing flat but it was a downer for everybody in the barrack to be quarantined for another two weeks.

They also gave us a flu shot and the whole cotton-picking barrack had the flu for a couple of days and we couldn't even pull our own guard duty. We were so sick we had to get another company to pull guard duty for us. It was the first flu shot I'd ever had and I've had one more since then and got sick again. I'll never take another flu shot for as long as I live.

Finally, they processed and released us and put us aboard the Smith Victory and sent us home. We hit some rough seas coming back, about as rough as they were going over. We had to button up and nobody was allowed out on deck. To button up means to lock down the hatches.

Most of the GI's on board were seasick. They were vomiting all over the place, but I never did show any effect of seasickness at all, so I ate good. I'd carry foodstuff down in the hole and they'd run me out. They'd shout, "Get the hell out of here," and they'd start heaving when they saw the food. I stayed down in the whole so long and smelling all that crap that I was determined to get out on deck. So I opened up the hatch and I went out on deck. It was so rough that I'd have to pick me a spot and run for it and grab it and hold on for a minute. Then when the ship leveled up a little bit I'd run and grab another spot. I finally made it to the bow of the ship. I'm sure that the pilot and his crew up there in the pilothouse saw me out on deck, but they didn't say nothing or holler at me or do anything about it.

I was leaning right over the bow and enjoying the porpoises. They were coming right up to me. I mean they were close enough that I could almost touch them, and then the whole bow of the ship went under water. I ducked underneath the bow and I got soaking wet. Then I worked my way back to the hole and went down. That little break with the fresh salty air and that good salt-water shower helped me a lot, but it's a wonder I didn't get washed overboard. Wouldn't that have been something? I survived the war but was washed over board just as we were getting into Boston Port? The storm went on for about seven days. We were right out of Boston and heading into the Boston Port. As we were trying to get in we were bucking the wind and the crew couldn't hold our position. The sailors were concerned about the wind backing us up into Cape Cod.

It finally cleared up and we went on into port and there were at least five boats that met us out in the port. All of them were pumping water and spraying it up in the air. It was a victory celebration of our homecoming. There was a big banner up on the side of a building saying, "Welcome Home". When we landed in Boston and I got off the ship, would you believe that the Red Cross gave us coffee and donuts and didn't charge us? I guess they don't charge when you're on American soil. "American soil" what a beautiful sound. I wanted to kiss the ground.

We were again assigned to some barracks and I had some extra clothes that I was going to bring home with me. I also had two or three extra pistols that I wasn't supposed to have. We were expecting a shakedown, but we didn't get one at that time. They put us on a troop train and I volunteered for guard duty on the mess car. We headed for Fort Knox, Kentucky.

In Fort Knox there was a Colonel greeting us when we got off the train. He was kind of an old fellow or at least I thought he was old. I was carrying two barrack's bags that were a pretty good load. The Colonel was welcoming us into the fort. He sounded like a real good Joe and I said, "Hey, Colonel. You going to the barracks with us?"

He said, "Yea."

I said, "Would you mind carrying one of these bags?"

He said, "Not at all." He grabbed one of them and carried the bag to the barracks for me.

We got in there and we hadn't even stretched our legs when someone hollered, "Shakedown!" Well, I raised the window and threw one of the bags out the window, but there were guys outside expecting that, so they picked my bag up. Then we had the shakedown but they didn't find my guns. I had clothes in the barracks bag that were all folded up and I had stuck the guns in between the clothes. I had received orders signed by Eisenhower's headquarters before leaving Europe that authorized me to bring home the German Luger, so I didn't have to hide it, but the other guns were not authorized.

The next morning I got a haircut and kind of cleaned up a little bit. I met with an Administration Officer to complete my discharge papers.

"I'd like to join the Army Reserve."

"Why?"

""Well, the way I figure it, after the way those Russians were acting in Europe we're liable to go to war with them any day. Maybe by being in the Reserve, I won't have to go back over."

"Okay, we'll do that paper work next. John, I need to you visit with the Doc."

"What for?"

"Well, I see hear that you were on limited duty. Go see the Doc for an evaluation and he can get you a pension."

"I don't want no damn pension!"

"Why not?"

"Any veteran who draws a pension is labeled disabled. I don't want anything to do with it. I don't want VA benefits or nothing. I've done my time now I just want to go home."

"Well, I can't make you take it, but you're making a big mistake."

"I may be but I don't want to be considered disabled when I'm perfectly fine."

The Officer said, "Well then, you can go home right now but you'll have to come back to receive your discharge."

I asked, "When am I going to be discharged?"

The Administrative Officer said, "Probably tomorrow."

I said, "If it's going to be tomorrow, I'll just stay." I didn't want to go home and have to come back, so, I stayed over one more night.

The date was December 9, 1945. I went in to get my discharge and there was a whole bunch of soldiers in this large room and I was the only one in there that wasn't wearing a tie. I had my blouse open, no tie on and had it stuck down in my pocket. My dog tags were hanging out of my pocket. I was about half way back in the room, when the Colonel came in. I recognized him as being the same person who helped me carry my bags into the barracks. He saw me as soon as he stepped into the room. He stepped up to a little ole podium and he said, "Okay fellows, this show will go on and you guys will get your discharge just as soon as that soldier back there puts his tie on," and he was pointing and looking straight at me.

I had to put my tie and dog tags on like fast like then he said, "Now we will proceed." I was kind of sloppy and must have stuck out like a sore thumb. We got our discharge and the ceremony and all that crap took way on up into the afternoon. The bus scheduled to go to Nashville had left at 4 o'clock. It was after four o'clock and I had missed the bus and wanted to go home right then.

I went through the barracks hollering, "Anybody want to go to Nashville tonight? Step out in the hall." Wasn't anything flat, I mean a bunch of them started stepping out and we had enough to charter a bus to go to Nashville. We all chipped in and went down to the bus station. Of course, I was the one that chartered the bus and made the arrangements. We got aboard the bus and we headed towards Nashville.

On the way home, it was raining and it was cold since it was December. There was a guy hitchhiking. I told the bus driver to pull over and pick up the hitchhiker, so he pulled over and picked the guy up. By this time, it was about nine thirty or ten at night. The hitchhiker sat down towards the back of the bus and started yak, yak, yaking, yak, yak, yaking, yak, yak, and yaking. I said, "Hey Bud, how about shutting up, these guys are asleep on here. Be quiet will ya?"

He said, "Okay, all right." After a few minutes he started yak, yak, and yaking again.

I was surprised he started talking that quickly and I said to him again, "Hey Bud, shut up. I told you to be quiet and
202

let them guys sleep." In just a few minutes he started yak, yak, and yaking again.

I couldn't believe it. So I got up this time and walked towards the back of the bus where he was sitting and got right beside him and looked him right in the eyes and said in as stern a voice as I could, "I told you to shut up!"

He shut up and I went back and sat down up in front but this time I got closer to the bus driver. Can you believe that in just two or three minutes after I got in his face and told him to shut up that he started yak, yak, and yaking again? I said to the bus driver, "Pull over," so the driver pulled over and stopped.

I said to the hitchhiker, "Hit the door, now!"

He said, "What? You going to put me off?"

I said, "You got it right, Bud," so I put his butt out.

When we drove off, that bus driver said, "I knew damn well you were going to do that. I knew it was working up to just that."

I got into Nashville about midnight and took a taxi home. I didn't want to wake Mary until I got home and besides that the car was still sitting in the garage. She hadn't driven it since she got that ticket more than two years earlier.

As I approached the house I could see the Christmas tree lights glowing from the living room window and there were other lights on in the house. I surprised Mary when I walked through the door. That was the greatest Christmas and the happiest day of my life. Mary screamed with excitement when she saw my face and I gave a quick, "Praise God, Thank you Jesus" and grabbed her and held her tight. I was afraid to let go. Afraid I might be dreaming and wake up in a field somewhere in Germany. It felt so good to have her in my arms again and to finally be home. We stayed up all night talking and making love. Either I've got a guardian angel watching over me or I'm the luckiest guy in the world.

I was happy to have serviced my country and now I was done and glad to be home.

Two days after I got home we had a visitor. Someone knocked at the door and when I opened it a man was standing on my front porch wearing a dark blue suit. He introduced himself, "Hello, I'm Agent Thomas, FBI."

As he flashed his identification card he asked, "May I come in?"

I hesitantly said, "Well, Okay what do you want? What are you here for?"

He said, "You are John C. Estes and you were recently discharged from the Army?"

I said, "Yea, that's true, you got it." After everything that went on in Europe, I didn't know what to expect next. I felt a lump form in my throat.

He said, "You brought a gun home with you?"

I said, "Yes."

He said, "What kind is it?"

I said, "It's a Luger." Of course, I didn't tell him about the three other guns.

He said, "May I see it?"

I said, "Yea, wait here and I'll get it." I went back in the bedroom, got the gun out of the holster and brought it to him as he stood in the living room. I didn't bring in the holster because I had a spare barrel down in the holster that I didn't want him to see. I handed him the gun. He looked at its serial number and checked it out pretty good.

Then he said, "Okay, Everything seems to check out. Now I've got to ask you a few questions. Where did you land when you came back from overseas?"

I said, "I landed in Boston, Mass then went to Fort Knox."

He said, "How did you travel from Boston to Fort Knox?"

"By troop train."

"Okay, when you were discharged at Fort Knox, how did you get on home?"

"I chartered a bus."

"Did you wear your uniform all the way home?"

"Yea, and why are you asking me all these questions?"

He said, "Well, we've got to because you brought a foreign gun into the United States. Because you crossed a couple of state lines we have to notify the state authorities that you crossed their state carrying a foreign gun. If they want to prosecute you, then they can."

I said, "Are you kidding me?!"

"No, that's the law, but don't get excited. Everything is okay because you wore your uniform all the way home, so they have no jurisdiction."

"So you mean, if I'd come home in my civilian clothes from Fort Knox, then Kentucky could have prosecuted me for carrying that gun across the state? And then Tennessee could also prosecute me?"

"Yep that's right. Now that you're home, then the pistol's at home and the state will allow it here." He stuck a swab looking thing up in the barrel and turned it and tightened it up and pulled it out. Then he put the swab into a little ole bag and turned around to leave. As he walked towards the door he turned and said, "If you ever use that gun to shoot somebody, we'll be able to match the bullet to that barrel. Merry Christmas," then he left.

I worked on the car the rest of the day and managed to get it started. The next day I drove over to the Nashville Bridge Company where I was rehired as a welder. After I had completed my employment paperwork, the administration clerk handed me a card to sign authorizing them to deduct a days pay as a contribution to the Red Cross.

He asked, "Would you like to donate a day's pay to the Red Cross through payroll deduction?"

I said, "Hell no!"

He looked puzzled and said, "Well, I've got to get you to sign the card anyway." I signed it and wrote across the top, "Not one damn penny."

He asked, "You sure you want this to go in like that?" He seemed really, really puzzled.

I said, "Yes sir," and got up and left the administrative office. Later that day the Superintend, Mr. Anderson, called me into his office to ask me about it.

"John, can you explain to me why you wrote this on the card and why you feel that way?"

I told him the story about having to buy food from the Red Cross when the Army was starving us when we first arrived in England and I told him about the time I was lost in London and didn't have any money and the Red Cross deducted the a room charge from my paycheck. He had a hard time believing that I had to pay one hundred dollars to the Red Cross to buy a train ticket to get Ruskie home. Thank goodness the guys chipped in or it would have cost me about six weeks pay.

"So you see Mr. Anderson, I'm not donating nothing. I didn't get anything from the Red Cross when I was overseas and they're not getting anything from me."

C - 15 658 409

Army of the United States

Honorable Discharge

This is to certify that

JOHN C. ESTES 34 884 357 **TECHNICIAN FIFTH GRADE,**

710TH ENGINEER COMBAT BATTALION DEPOT COMPANY

Army of the United States

is hereby Honorably Discharged from the military service of the United States of America.

This certificate is awarded as a testimonial of Honest and Faithful Service to this country.

Given at   SEPARATION CENTER
FORT KNOX, KENTUCKY

Date   9 DECEMBER 1945

APPLICATION FOR
READJUSTMENT ALLOWANCE
PUBLIC LAW #346
MADE THROUGH
STATE *Tennessee*
DATE

A. J. BALL
MAJOR, CAV

207

ENLISTED RECORD AND REPORT OF SEPARATION

HONORABLE DISCHARGE

1. LAST NAME - FIRST NAME - MIDDLE INITIAL	2. ARMY SERIAL NO.	3. GRADE	4. ARM OR SERVICE	5. COMPONENT
ESTES JOHN C	34 884 357	TEC 5	CE	AUS

6. ORGANIZATION	7. DATE OF SEPARATION	8. PLACE OF SEPARATION		
710 ENGR COMBAT BN DEPOT CO	9 DEC 45	SEPARATION CENTER FT KNOX KY		

9. PERMANENT ADDRESS FOR MAILING PURPOSES	10. DATE OF BIRTH	11. PLACE OF BIRTH		
1522 23RD AVE NASHVILLE DAVIDSON TENN	22 JUN 23	SMITHVILLE TENN		

12. ADDRESS FROM WHICH EMPLOYMENT WILL BE SOUGHT	13. COLOR EYES	14. COLOR HAIR	15. HEIGHT	16. WEIGHT	17. NO. DEPEND.
SEE 9	BRN	BLA	5' 9"	149 LBS.	2

18. RACE		19. MARITAL STATUS	20. U.S. CITIZEN	21. CIVILIAN OCCUPATION AND NO.
WHITE X	NEGRO OTHER (specify)	SINGLE X MARRIED OTHER (specify)	YES X NO	WELDER ARC 4-85.020

MILITARY HISTORY

22. DATE OF INDUCTION	23. DATE OF ENLISTMENT	24. DATE OF ENTRY INTO ACTIVE SERVICE	25. PLACE OF ENTRY INTO SERVICE
28 AUG 43		18 SEP 43	FT OGLETHORPE GA

26. SELECTIVE SERVICE DATA	26a. REGISTERED	27. LOCAL S.S. BOARD NO.	28. COUNTY AND STATE	29. HOME ADDRESS AT TIME OF ENTRY INTO SERVICE
X		8	DAVIDSON TENN	SEE 9

30. MILITARY OCCUPATIONAL SPECIALTY AND NO.	31. MILITARY QUALIFICATION AND DATE (i. e., infantry, aviation and marksmanship badges, etc.)
TRUCK DRIVER LIGHT 345	SHARPSHOOTER RIFLE M1

32. BATTLES AND CAMPAIGNS
NORMANDY NORTHERN FRANCE ARDENNES RHINELAND CENTRAL EUROPE

33. DECORATIONS AND CITATIONS
GOOD CONDUCT MEDAL WORLD WAR II VICTORY MEDAL
EUROPEAN-AFRICAN-MIDDLE EASTERN THEATER RIBBON WITH 5 BRONZE SERVICE STARS

34. WOUNDS RECEIVED IN ACTION
NONE

35. LATEST IMMUNIZATION DATES					36.	37. SERVICE OUTSIDE CONTINENTAL U. S. AND RETURN		
SMALLPOX	TYPHOID	TETANUS	OTHER (specify)			DATE OF DEPARTURE	DESTINATION	DATE OF ARRIVAL
20 OCT 43	28 AUG 43	21 APR 45	TYPHUS 19 APR 44			5 APR 44	EAME	19 APR 44
						19 NOV 45	USA	1 DEC 45

38. TOTAL LENGTH OF SERVICE					39. HIGHEST GRADE HELD
CONTINENTAL SERVICE		FOREIGN SERVICE			TECHNICIAN
YEARS	MONTHS	DAYS	YEARS	MONTHS	DAYS	5TH GRADE
0	6	25	1	7	27	

40. PRIOR SERVICE
NONE

41. REASON AND AUTHORITY FOR SEPARATION
CONVENIENCE OF THE GOVERNMENT RR1-1 (DEMOBILIZATION) AND AR 615-365 15

For convenience, a certificate of eligibility no. 2390-IXX has been
issued by the Veterans Administration to be used for the future request
of any guaranty or insurance benefit under Title III of the Servicemen's
Readjustment Act of 1944, as amended, that may be available to the
person to whom this separation certificate was issued.

42. SERVICE SCHOOLS ATTENDED	43.	EDUCATION (Years)
NONE	GRAMMAR 8	HIGH SCHOOL 14	COLLEGE 0

PAY DATA

44. LONGEVITY FOR PAY PURPOSES			45. MUSTERING OUT PAY		46. SOLDIER DEPOSIT ALT, TRAVEL PAY	47. TOTAL AMOUNT, NAME OF DISBURSING OFFICER
YEARS	MONTHS	DAYS	TOTAL	THIS PAYMENT		
2	3	12	$300	$100	NONE $10 90	194 04 F M BUKER MAJ FD

INSURANCE NOTICE

IMPORTANT IF PREMIUM IS NOT PAID WHEN DUE OR WITHIN THIRTY-ONE DAYS THEREAFTER, INSURANCE WILL LAPSE. MAKE CHECKS OR MONEY ORDERS PAYABLE TO THE
TREASURER OF THE U. S. AND FORWARD TO COLLECTIONS SUBDIVISION, VETERANS ADMINISTRATION, WASHINGTON 25, D. C.

48. KIND OF INSURANCE	49. HOW PAID	50. Effective Date of Allotment Discontinuance	51. Date of Next Premium Due (One month after 50)	52. PREMIUM DUE EACH MONTH	53. INTENTION OF VETERAN TO
Nat. Serv. X U.S. Govt. None	Allotment Direct to V.A. X	31 DEC 45	31 JAN 46	$6 50	Continue Discontinue Only X

54. REMARKS (This space for completion of above items or entry of other items specified in W. D. Directives)
ASR 2 SEP 45 78 INACTIVE SERVICE ERC 28 AUG 43 THRU 17
LAPEL BUTTON ISSUED TIME LOST UNDER AW 107 NONE SEP 43

55. SIGNATURE OF PERSON BEING SEPARATED	56. PERSONNEL OFFICER (Type name, grade and organization - signature)
John C. Estes	F B CURRICK 1ST LT CAV

WD AGO FORM 53-55
1 November 1944

This form supersedes all previous editions of
WD AGO Forms 53 and 55 for enlisted persons
entitled to an Honorable Discharge, which
will not be used after receipt of this revision

208

Epilogue

Calvin worked at the Nashville Bridge Company for approximately six months after returning home from the war when he decided to open Calvin's Grocery. He sold it one year later and worked for a trucking company. He was making deliveries to service stations and ran across one that was for sale and brought it after driving the delivery trucks for only six months. The station was named Calvin's Pan Am Service Station where one could buy gas and he had a full service auto maintenance garage. He sold the service station in 1948 because he received an offer to go to work for the TVA (Tennessee Valley Authority) which offered him a reasonable salary and excellent benefits. He worked at the TVA from 1948 until he retired in 1983. His final position was that of Yard Supervisor where he was responsible for all outside operations including heavy equipment, locomotives, cranes, bull dozers, etc. TVA flew him all over the country as an equipment evaluator. He had an average of 76 union employees reporting to him. These employees were members of IBEW and the Teamsters. He supervised a wide range of employees from hod carrier laborers to operating engineers.

Early in 1951 a buddy of his that was working at the Army Reserve headquarters telephoned him to let him know that he was cutting his papers to call him up. The Army was sending him to Texas. Texas is where they were forming a unit to send to Korea. Calvin spoke to a neighbor who lived across the street about joining the Air National Guard. He immediately joined the Air National Guard because it was a more active unit than the Army and less likely to be called up. He wanted to join before he received the papers from the Army. Thirty days after joining the Air National Guard he was activated. He had the highest number of service points in the entire division which included the southern states and went all the way up the eastern coast to Pennsylvania. Because of this he was able to pick his location and he chose Berry Field in Nashville. After fifteen months all veterans received a letter that they could be discharged. However, when he was discharged he had to go back in to the Army Reserve. The TVA transferred him to Stevenson, Alabama. He wrote the Army Adjutant General requesting a discharge for reasons of "leaving the state of Tennessee". He received that discharge and moved to Alabama. After living in Stevenson for a couple of years and on September 5, 1955, the TVA transferred him to the steam plant in Gallatin, TN In 1962, he and Mary purchased a house on Old Hickory Lake in the Gallatin area.

I guess because of time and money and maybe because it didn't seem necessary, he never officially adopted my mother who is only seven years younger than him. As I grew up my family spent most of the summer on the lake swimming, boating, water skiing and fishing. It is at this house where I remember hearing the "War Stories" as a child. Calvin and Mary lived there together for thirty-six years and until she passed away in 1998. On October 8, 1998, Viola was visiting and according to Calvin, Viola had made a real good dinner of chicken and dumplings. After eating, Mary lay down to take a nap and never woke up. Mary and Calvin were married a total of fifty-six years.

My father had passed away in 1997, so after Mary's death, Calvin and my mother, Viola purchased a house in Hartselle, Alabama, where they live today. However, Calvin refuses to sell the lake house in Gallatin and still calls it home. That's great for me, my brother and sisters, because September 9, 1999 Calvin officially adopted my mother, Viola, becoming legally related. Therefore, all his possessions will pass down to my mother, then me and my siblings. Calvin says that Viola is the best nurse anyone could ask for and he loves her very much.

As I come to the end of Memorial Road, John Calvin Estes had been battling cancer for several years and at the age of 87 the doctors pretty much told him to forget the treatments and enjoy the remainder of his time here on earth. For a while the cancer kept him nauseated and unable to eat. During that time, he lost so much weight that he looked similar to the Jewish prisoners in the concentration camps he liberated so many years ago. Near the end, he had trouble keeping food down and finally lost his battle on September 10, 2010. I'm sure that when Calvin took his ride on God's soul train to heaven he volunteered to be the guard in the mess car where I'm sure he received plenty of food for his soul.

CPSIA information can be obtained at www.ICGtesting.com
Printed in the USA
LVOW071627100312

272513LV00003B/1/P